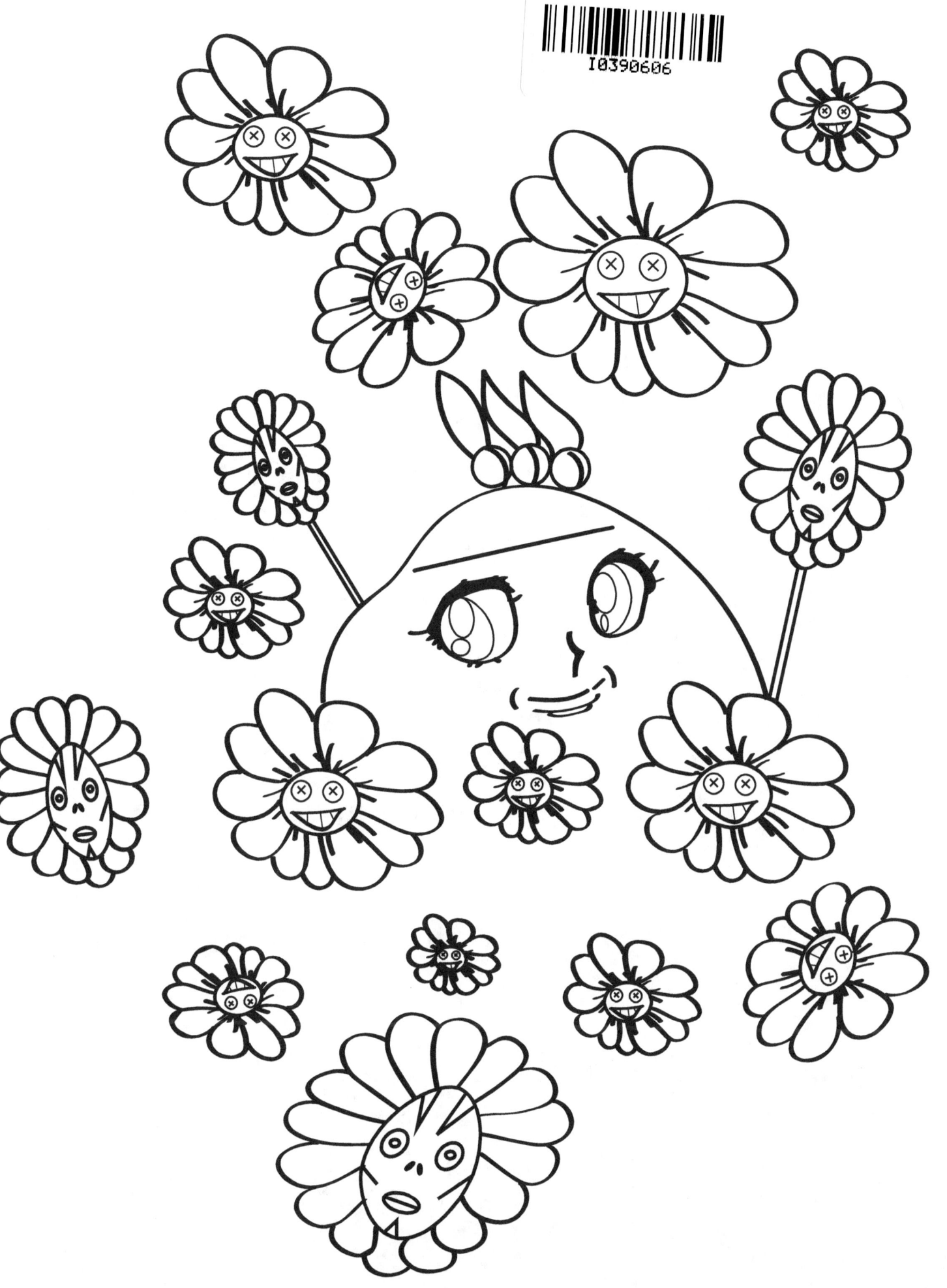

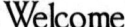

Welcome

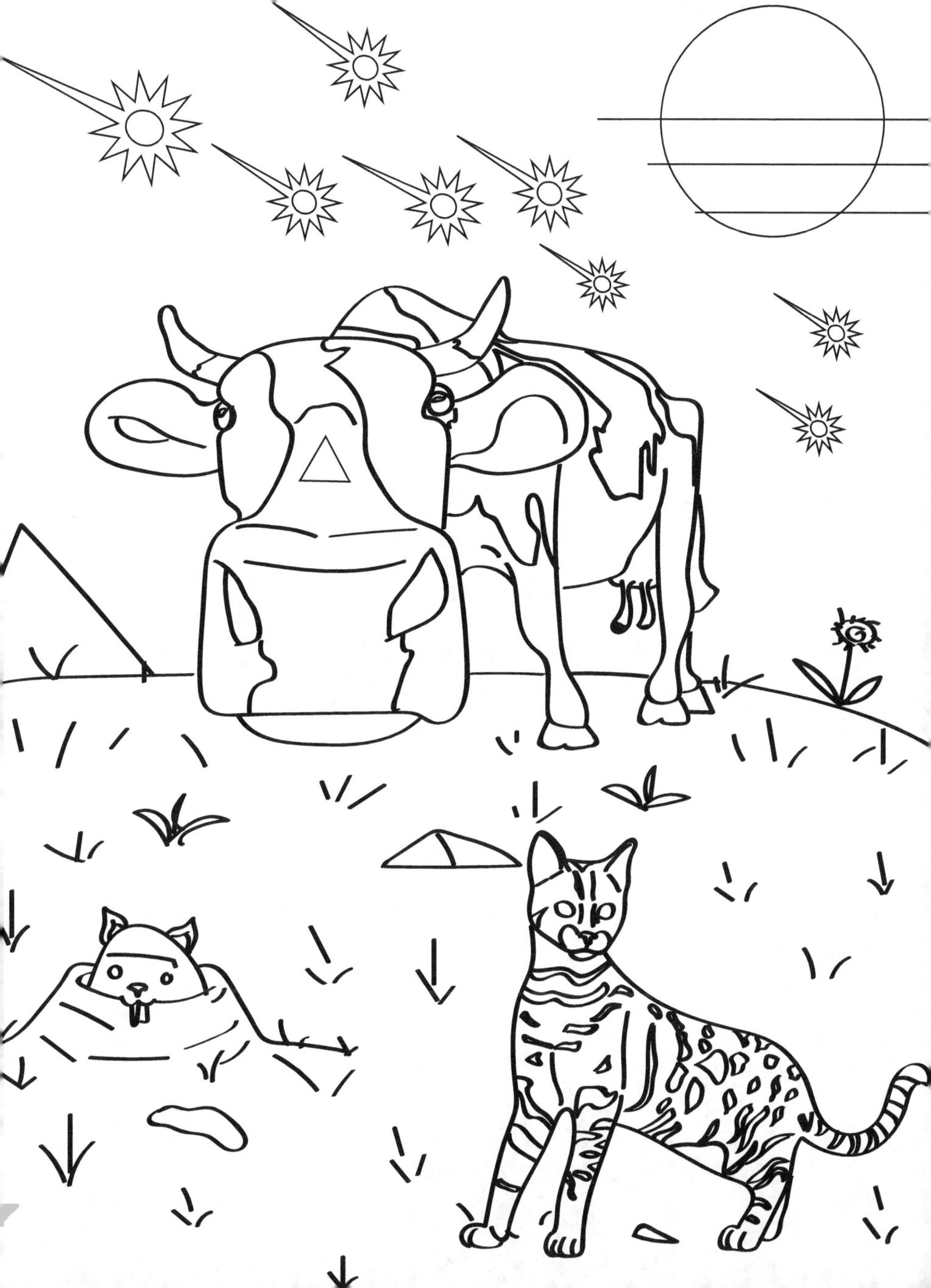

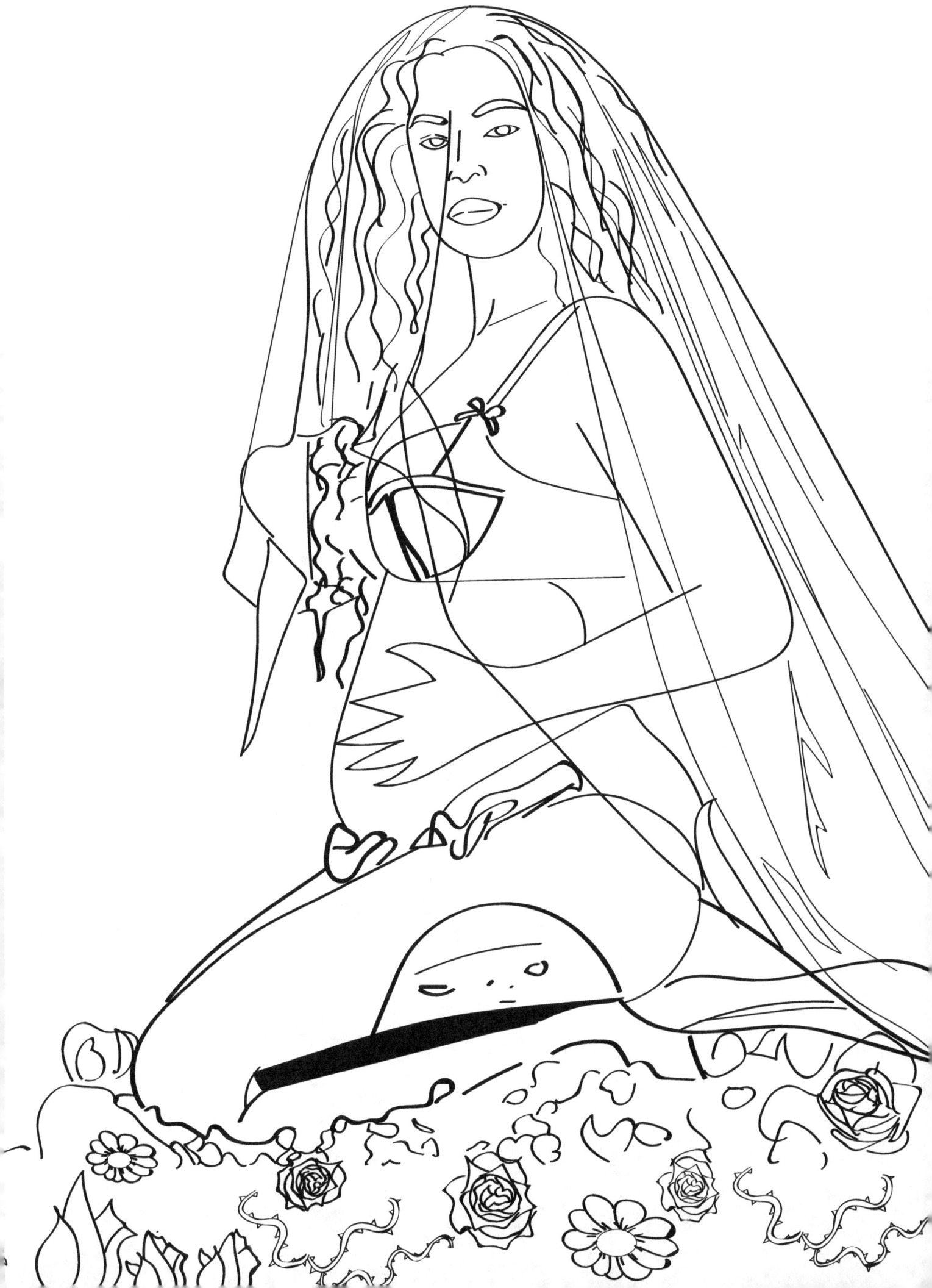

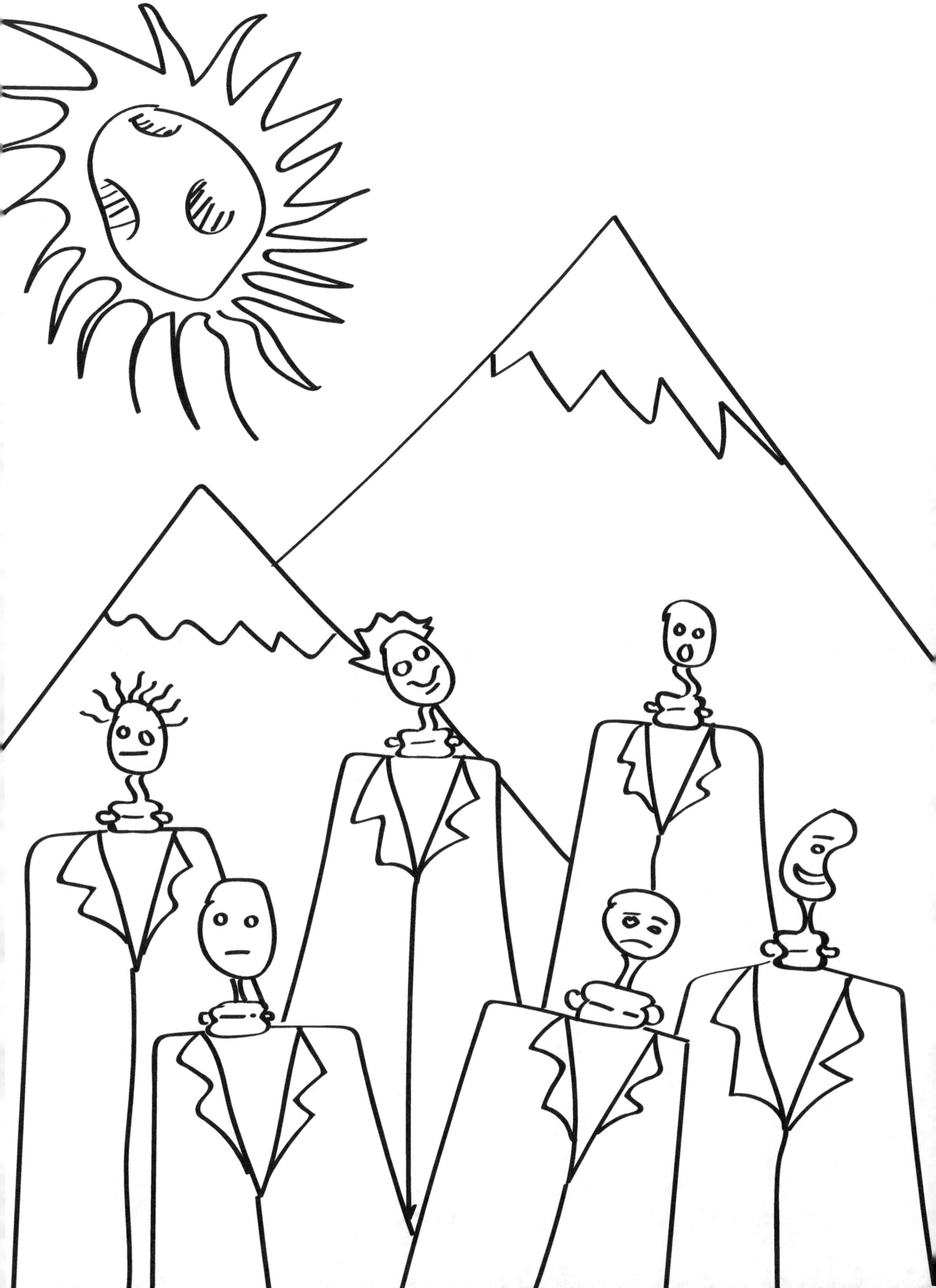

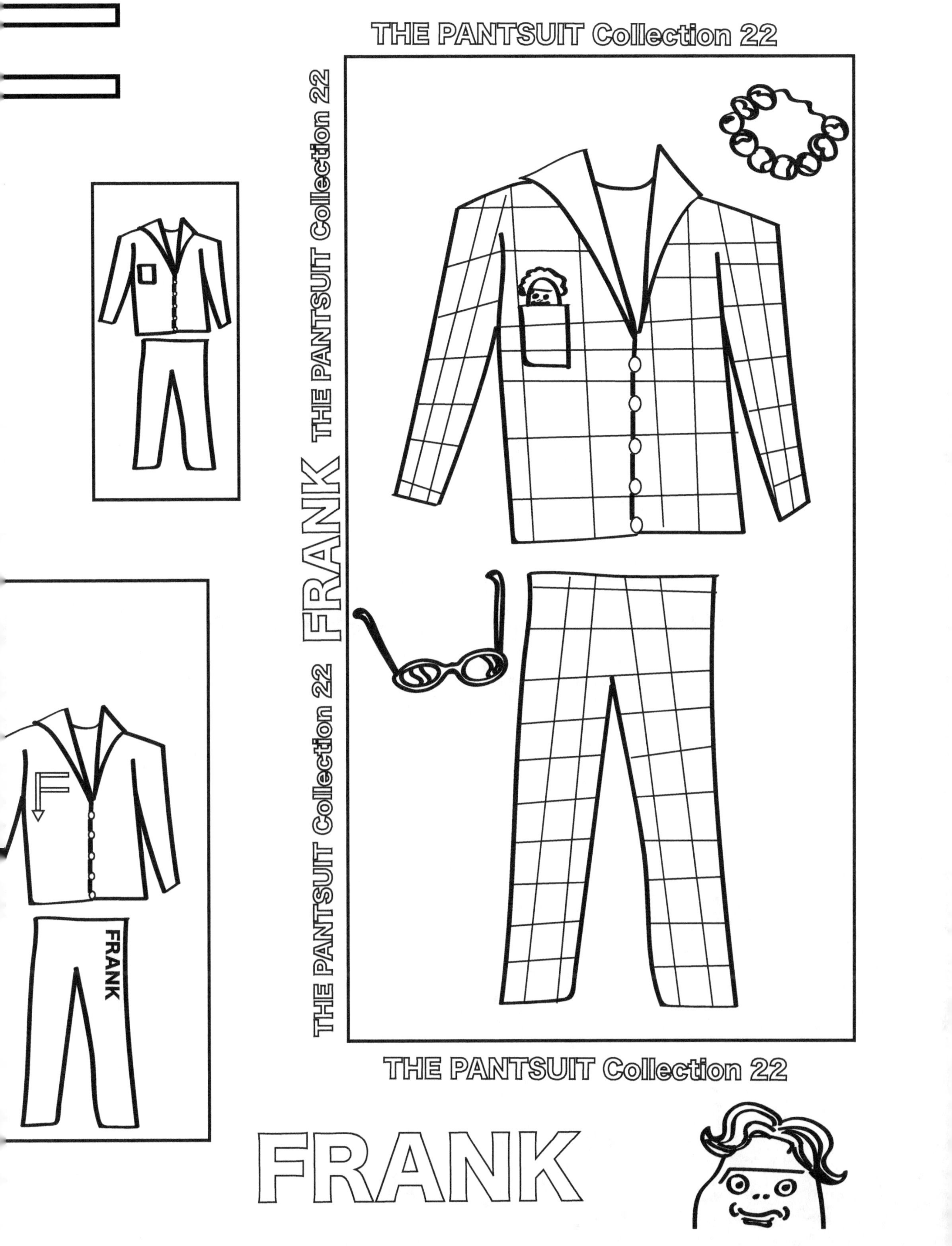

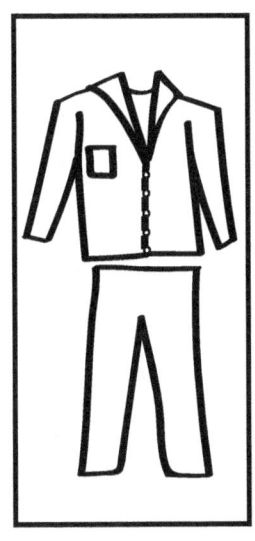

FRANK THE PANTSUIT Collection 22

THE PANTSUIT Collection 22

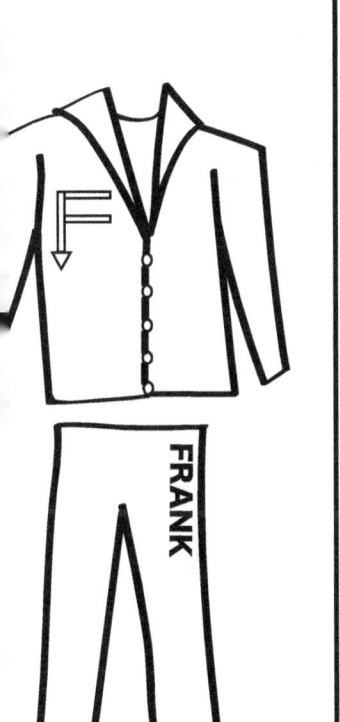

FRANK

THE PANTSUIT Collection 22

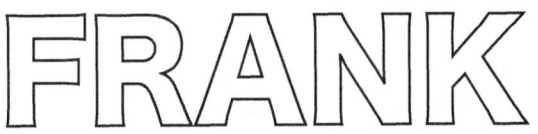

FRANK

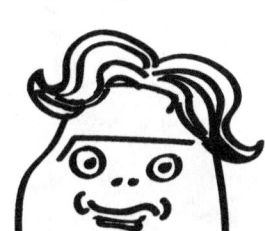

Starlight by the Sunset

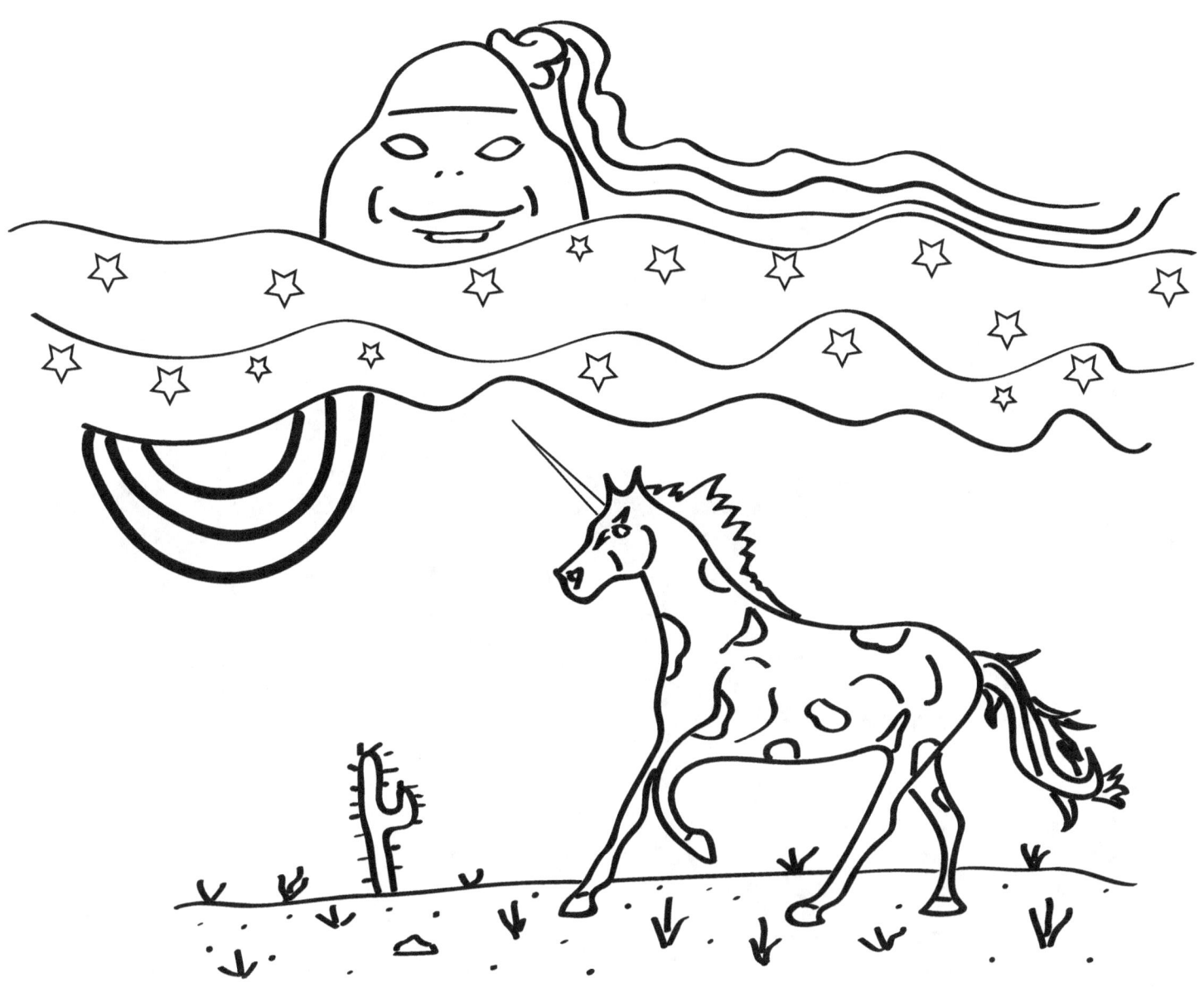

The Cold Wind Around U

The Cold Wind Around U

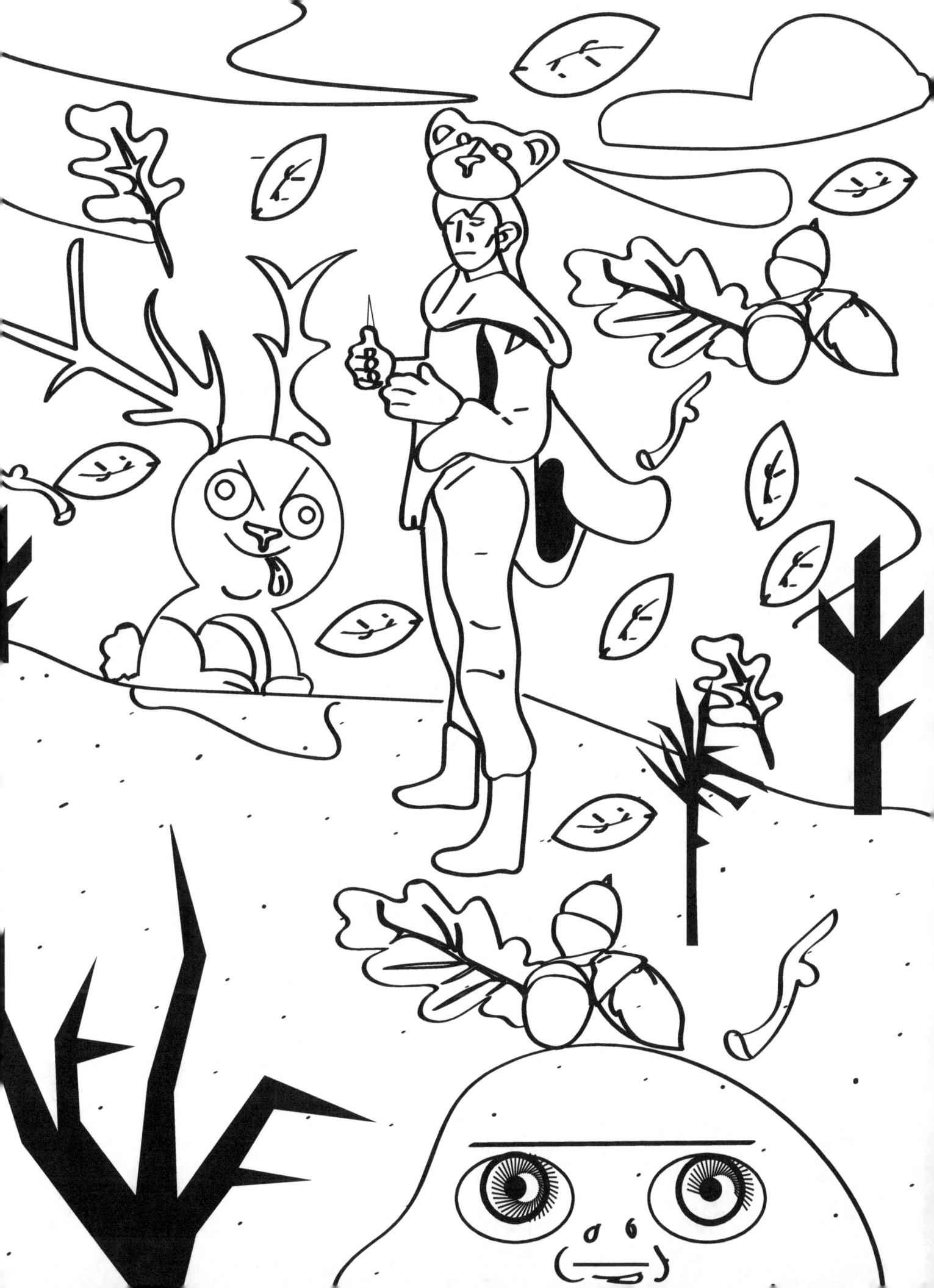

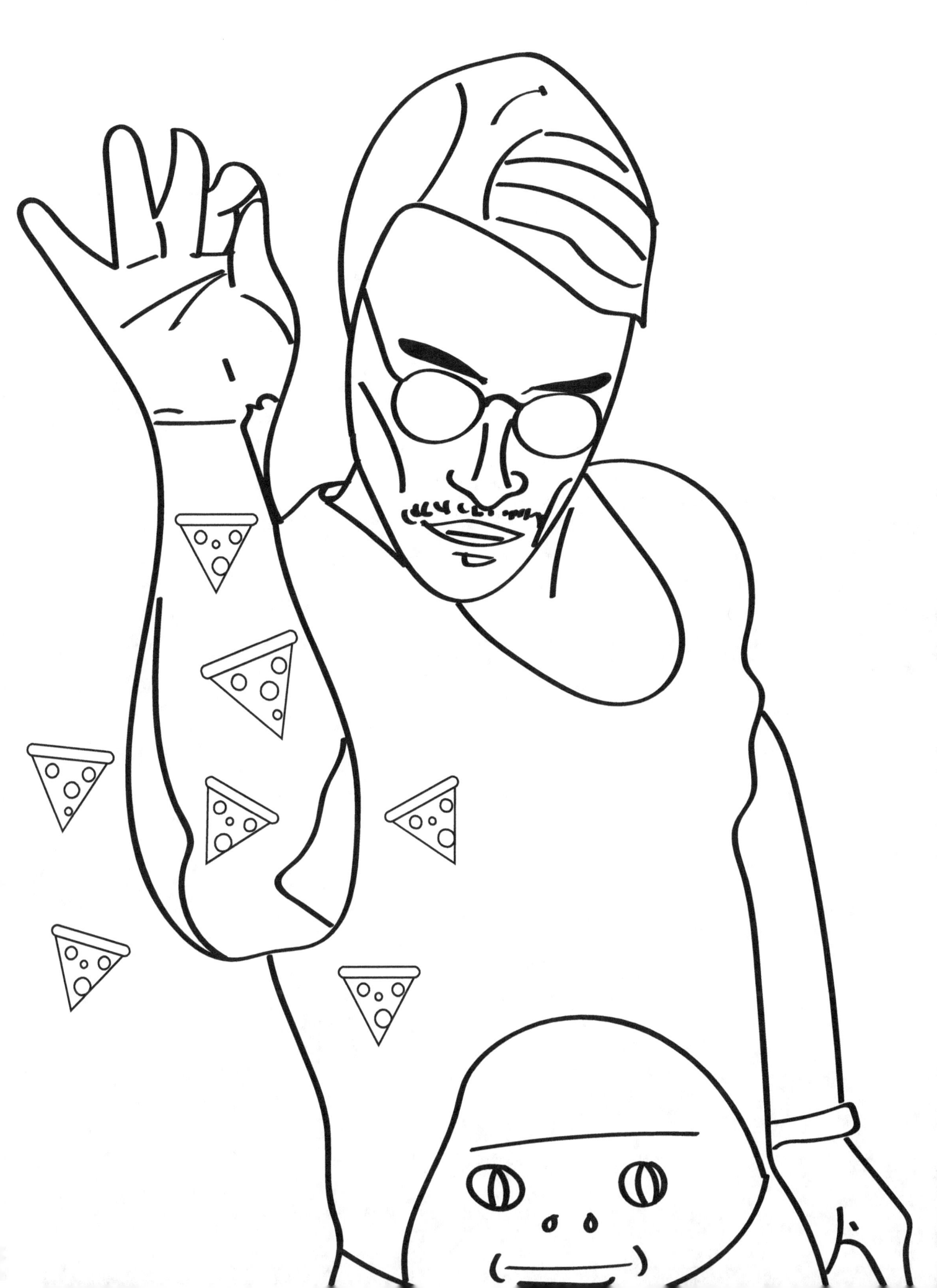

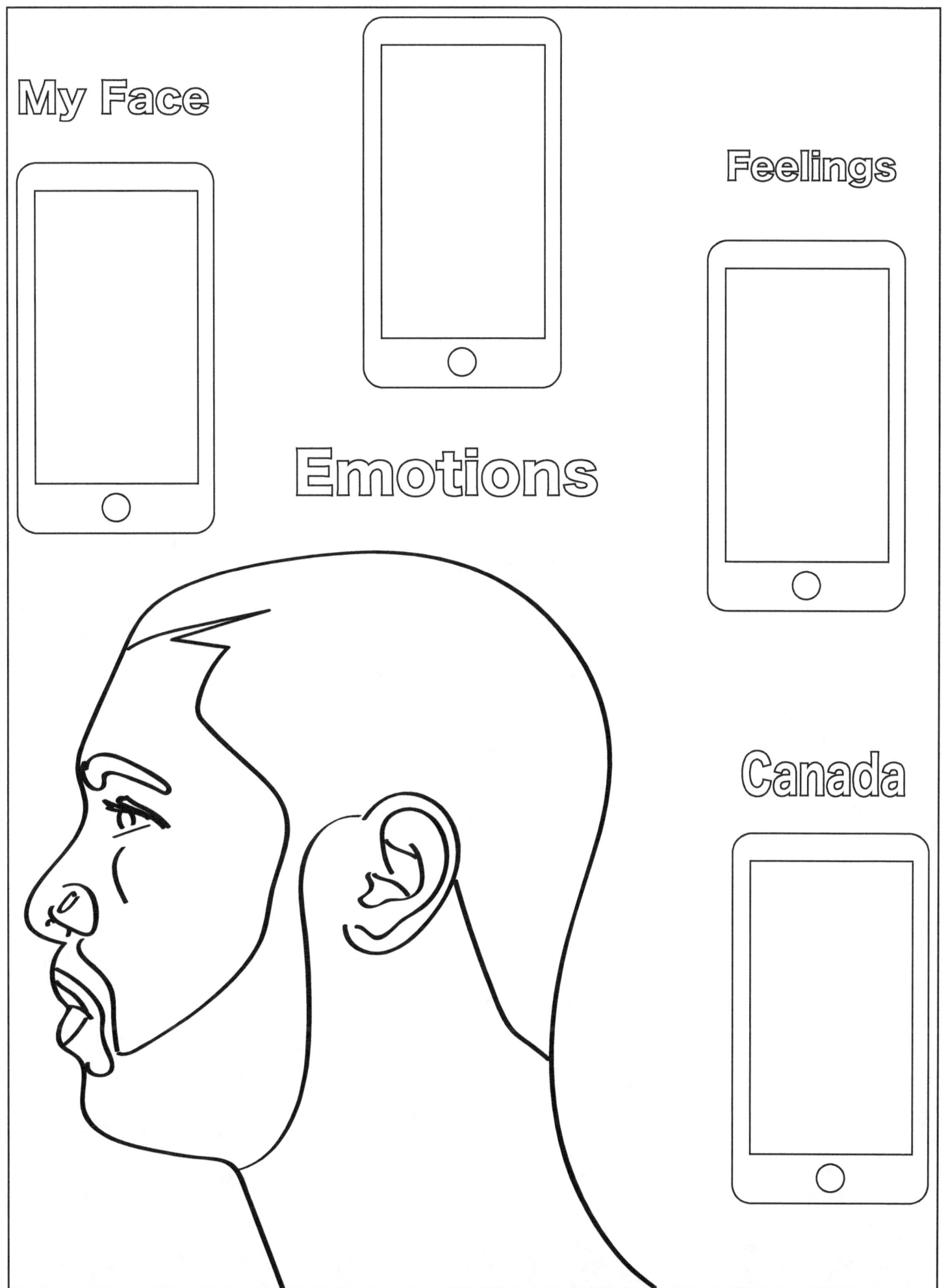

My Face

Feelings

Emotions

Canada

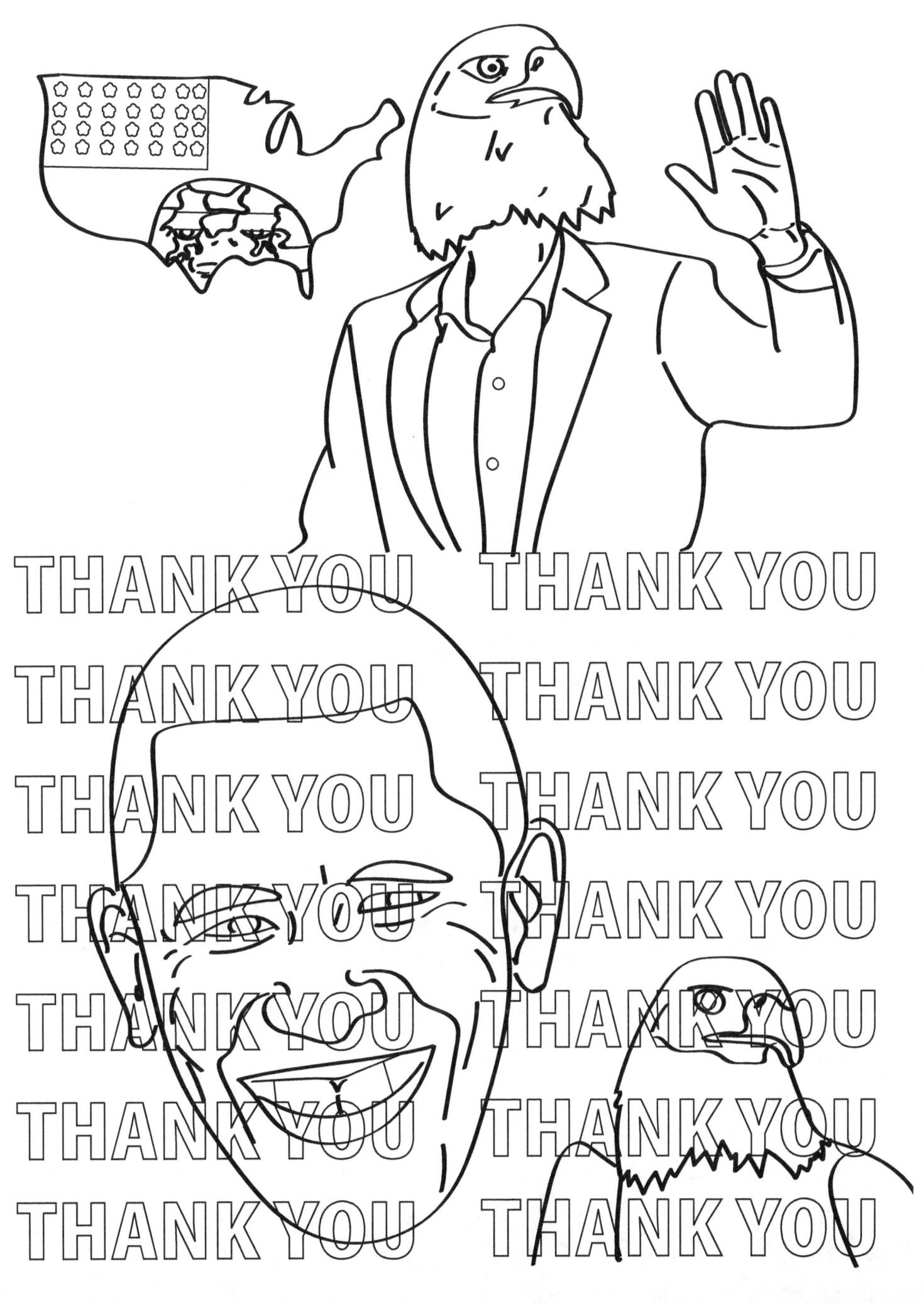

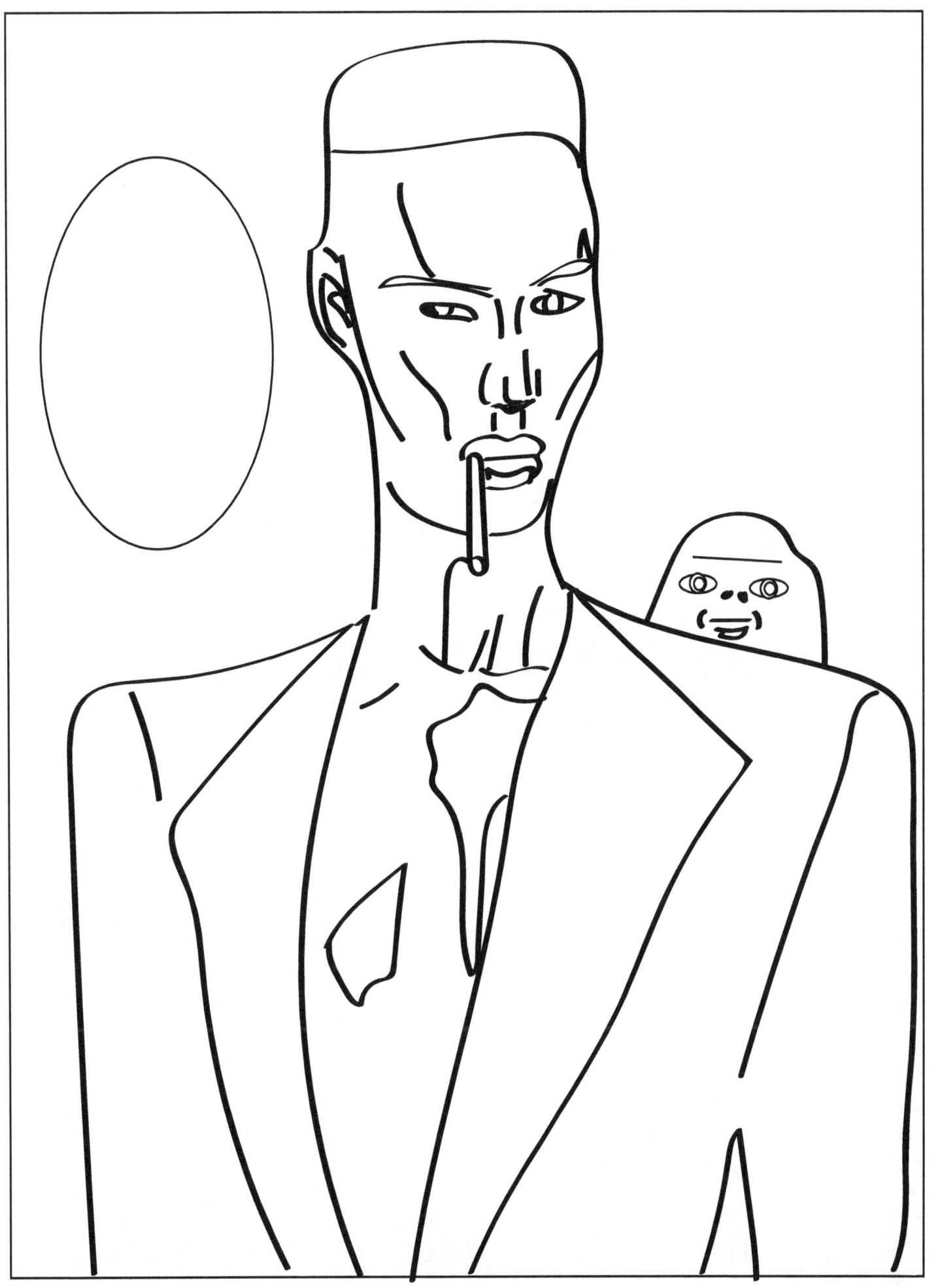

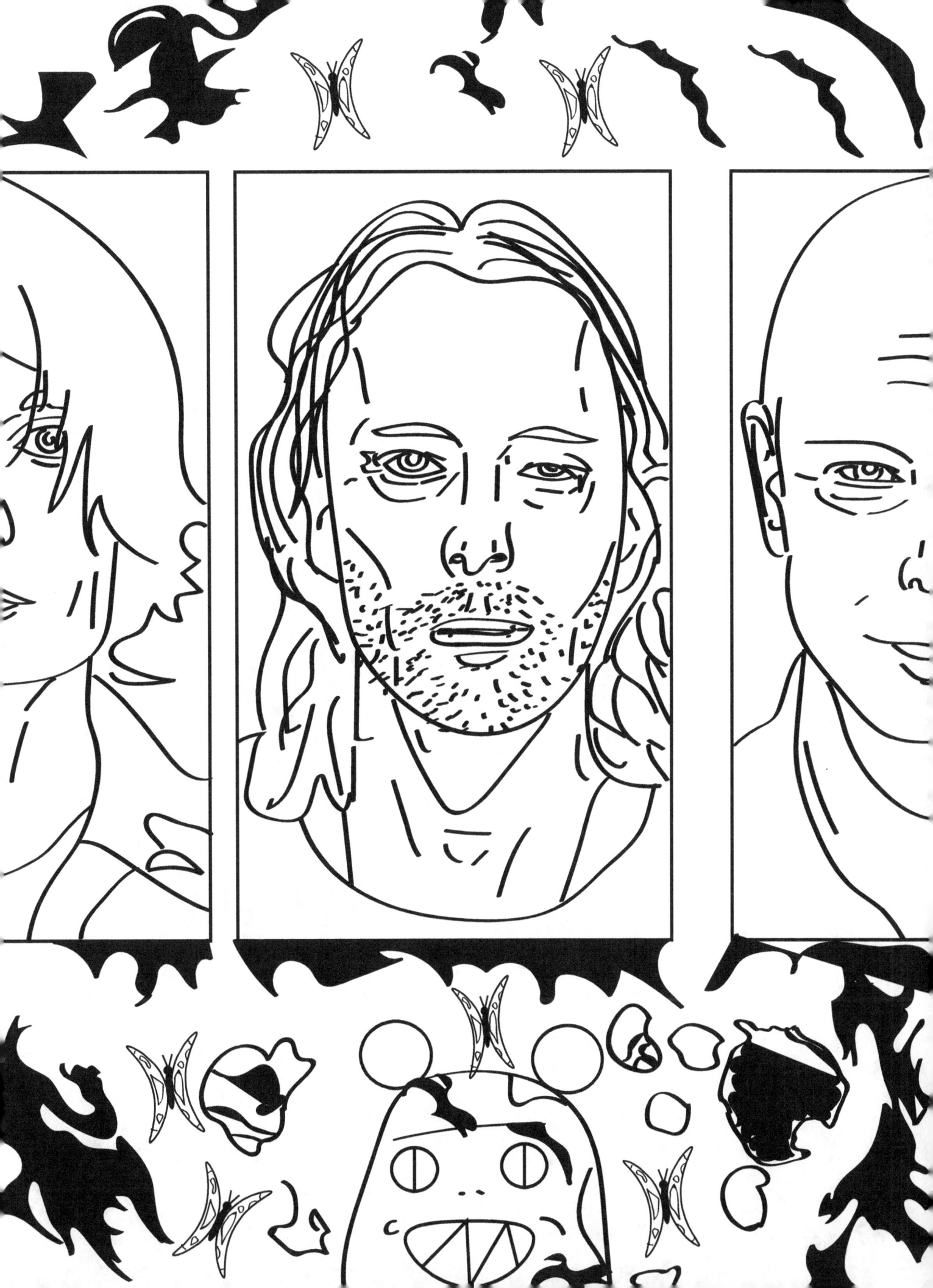

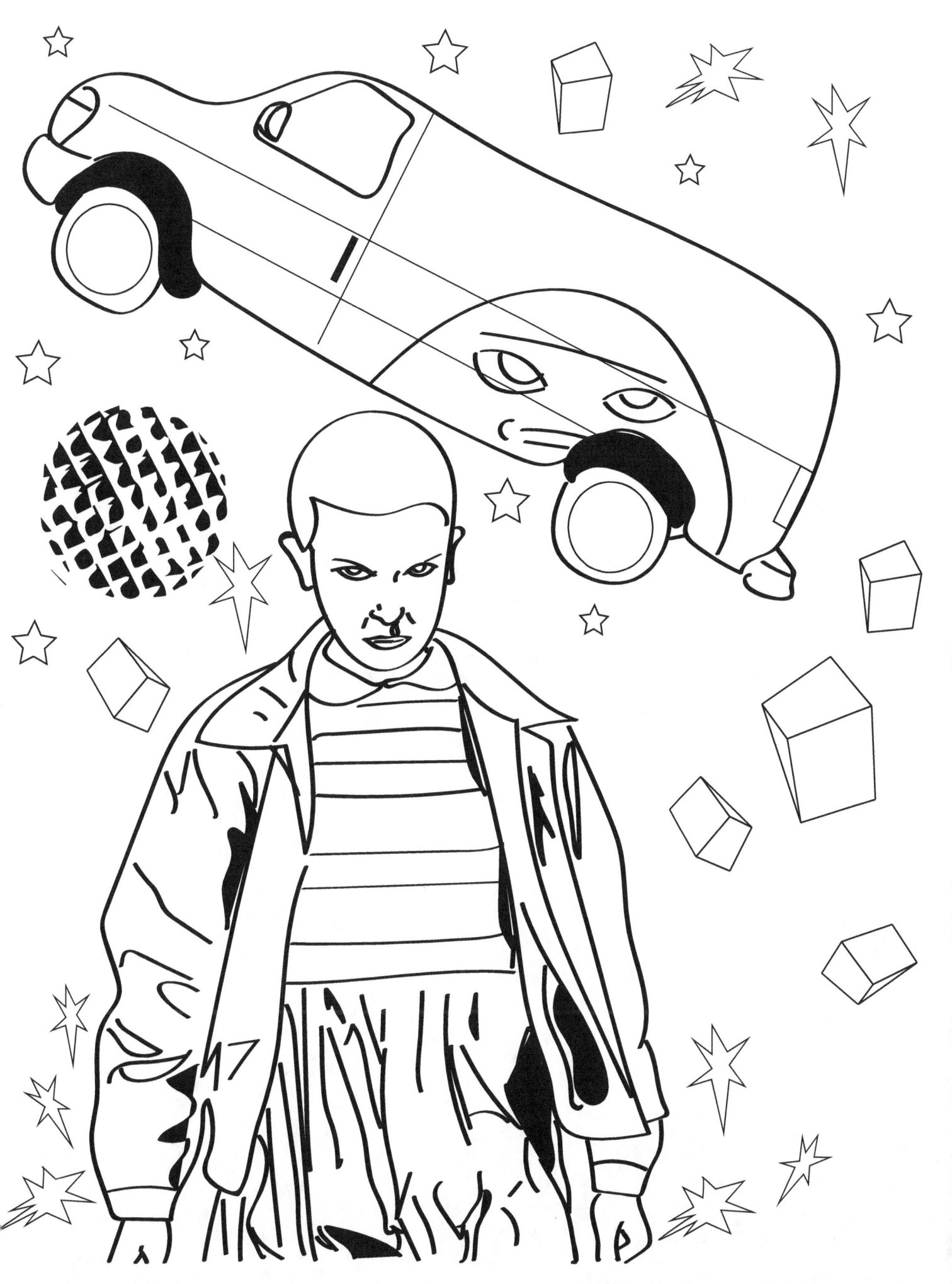

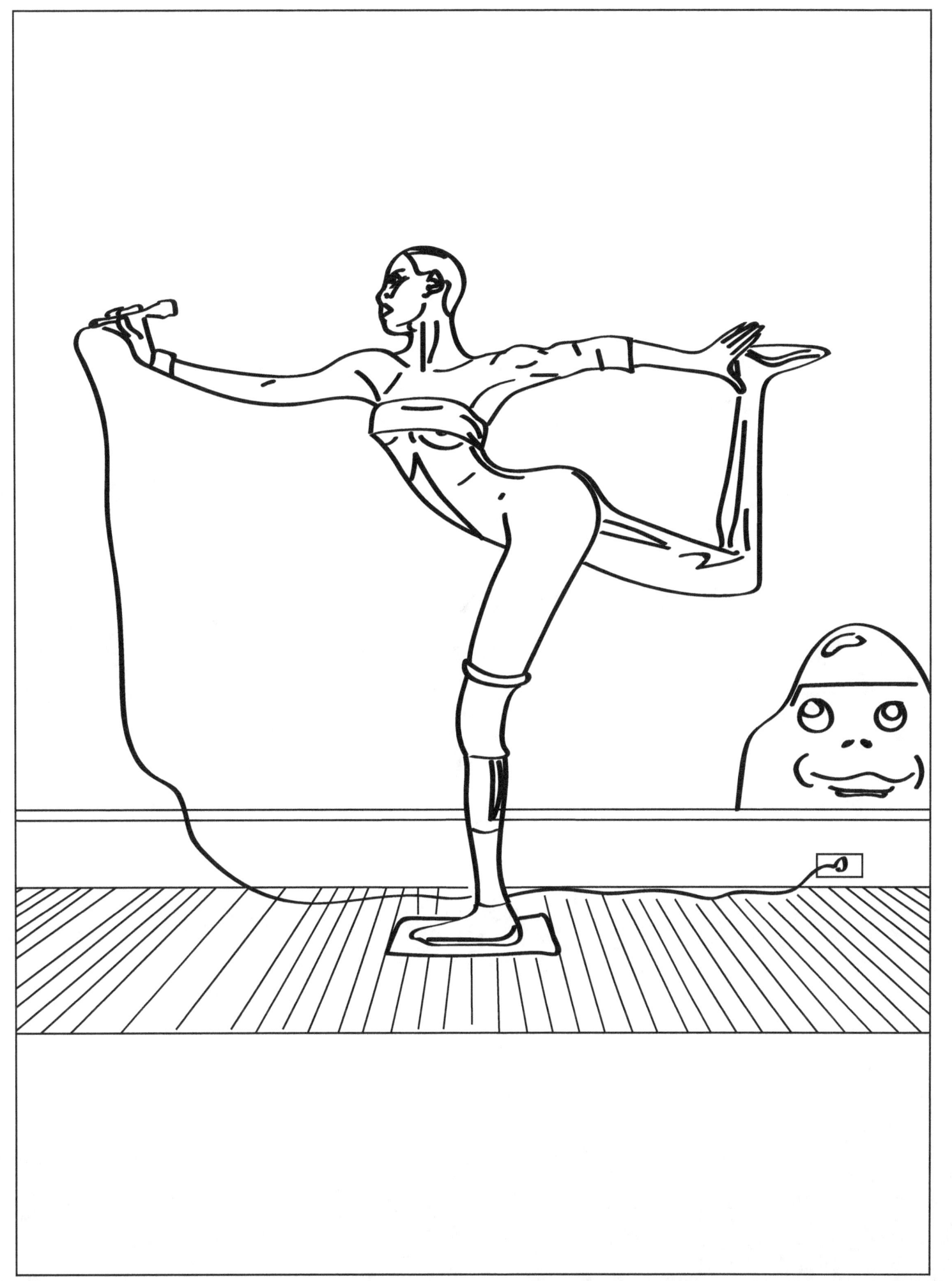

An Abstract View of the Table

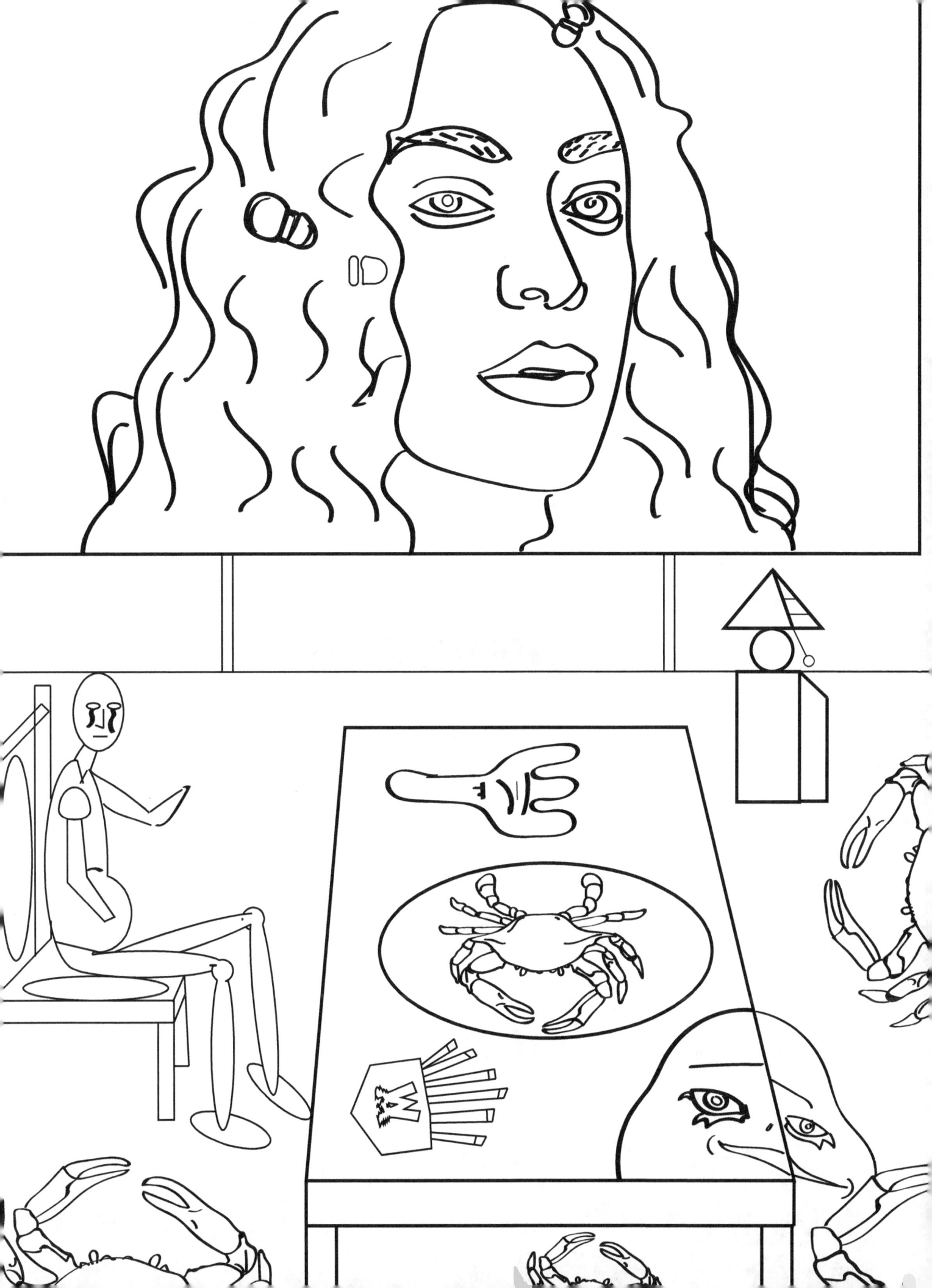

Amoureuse

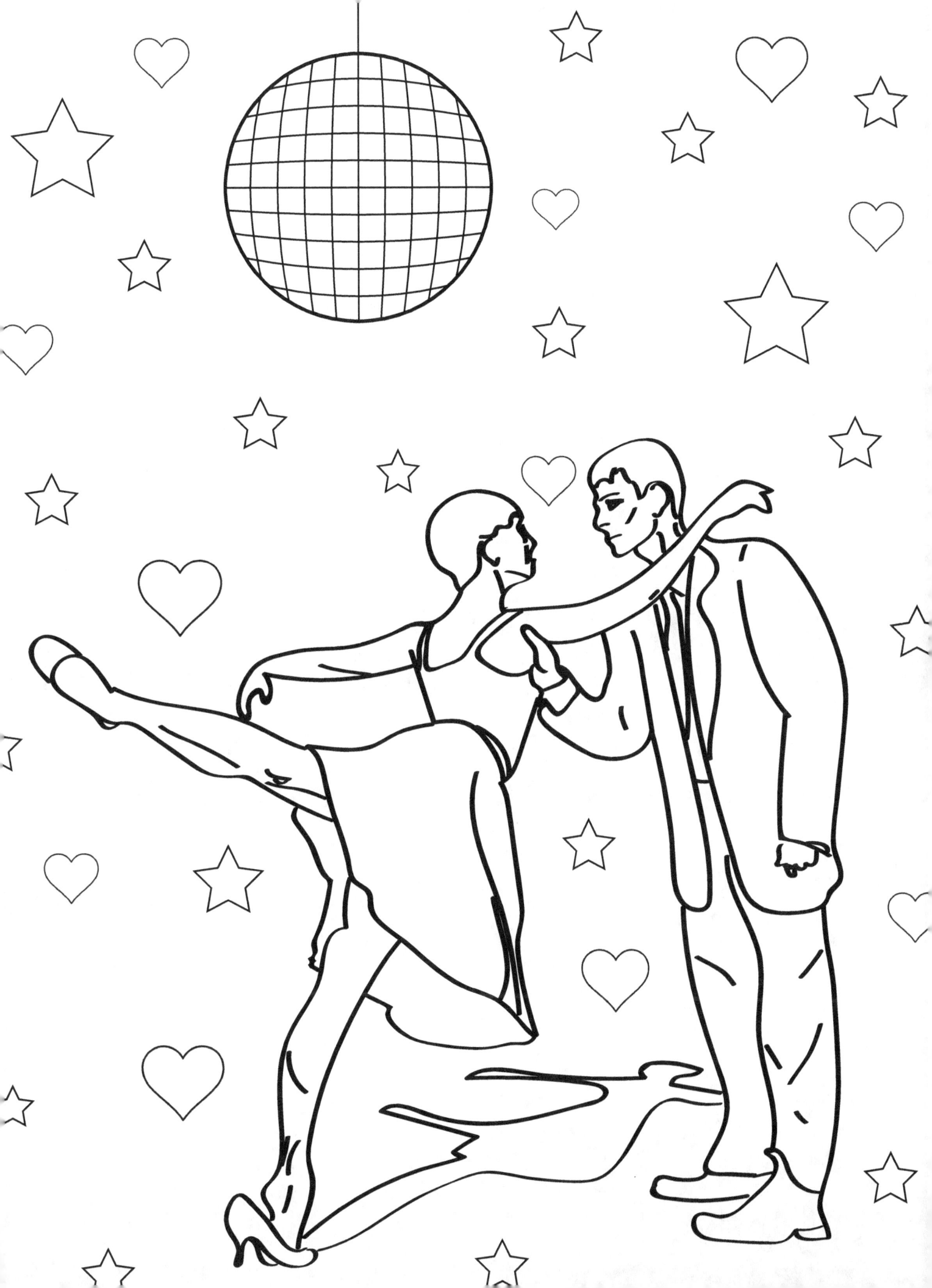

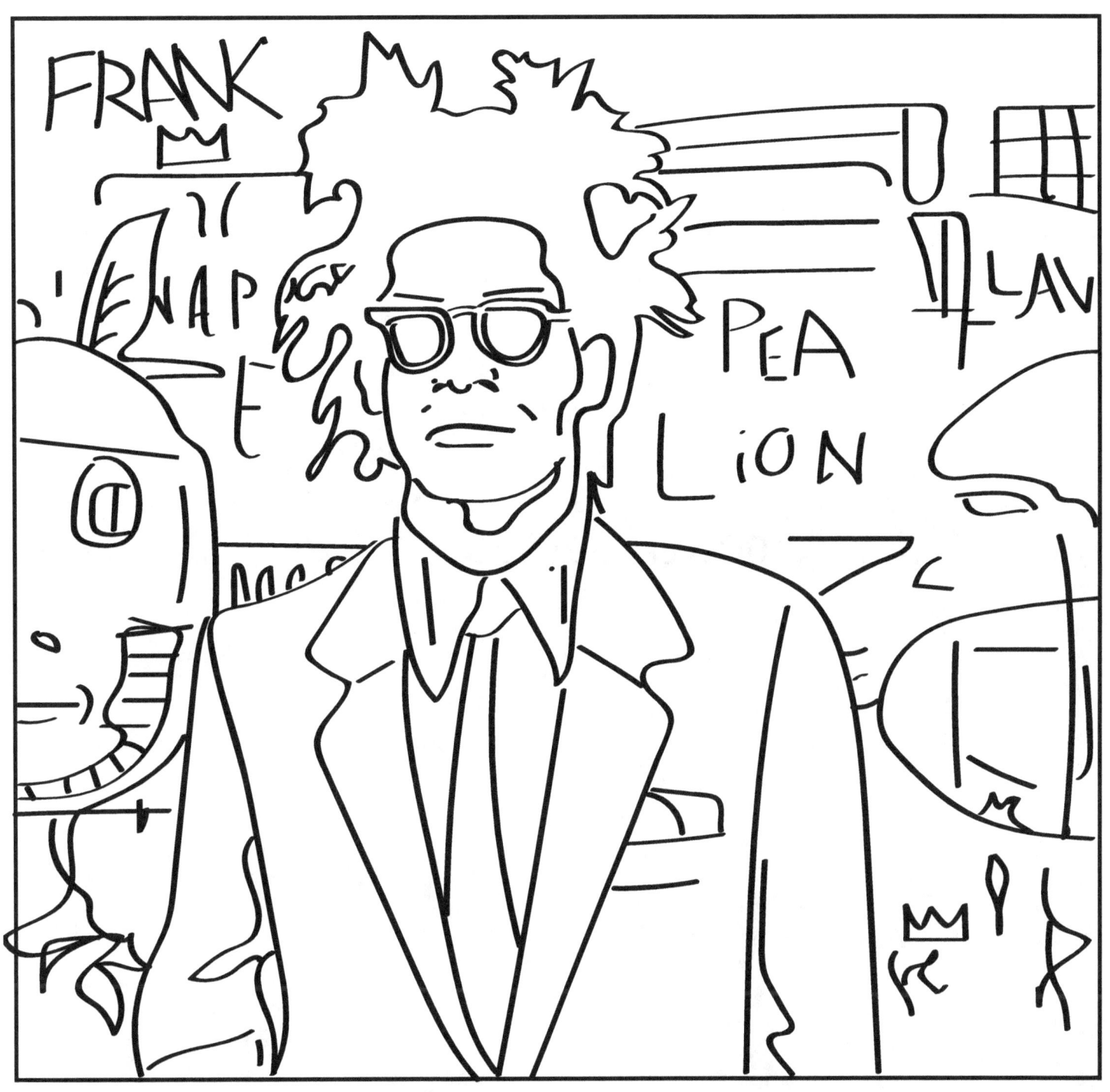

Ghetto Blasted

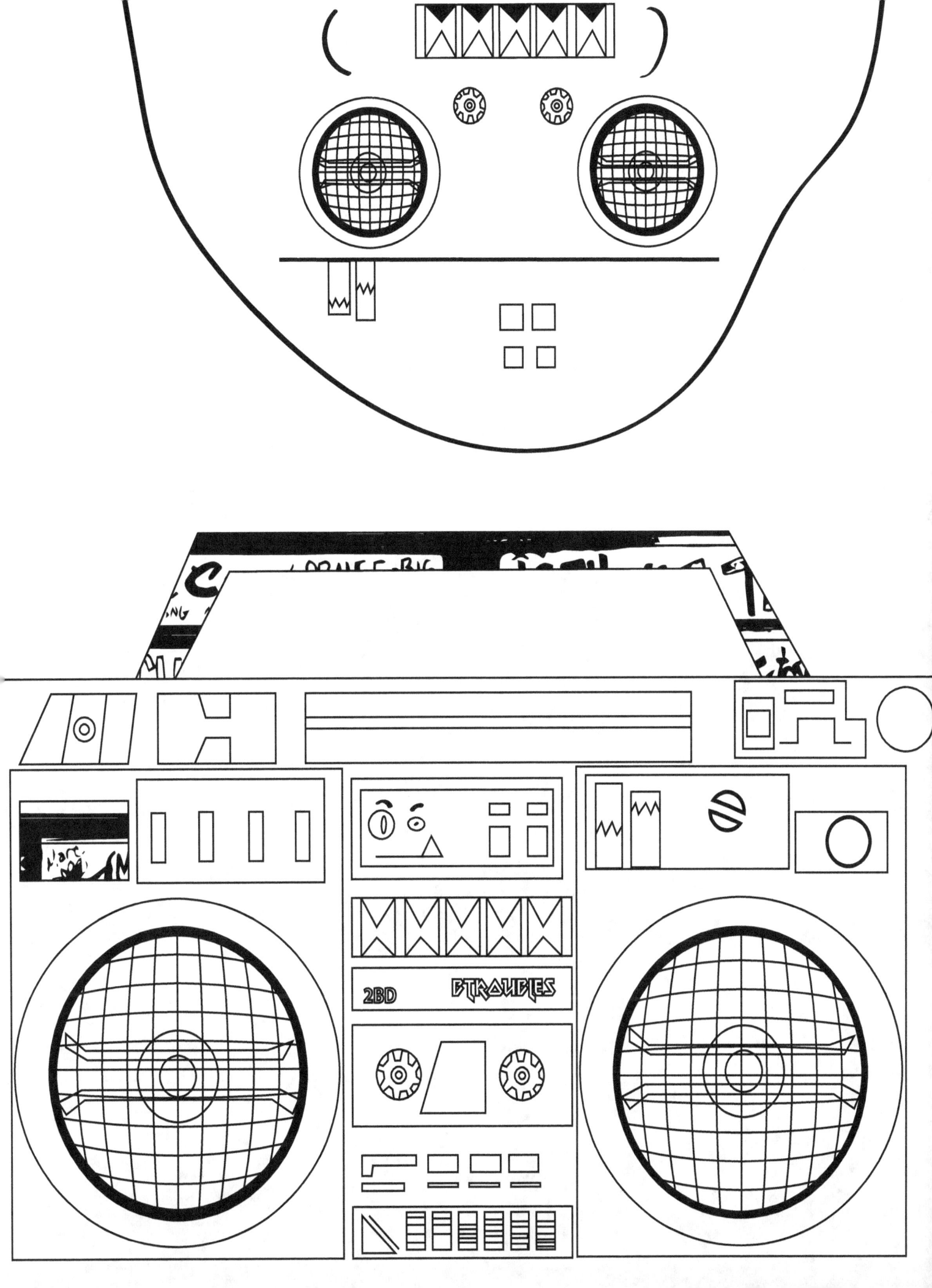

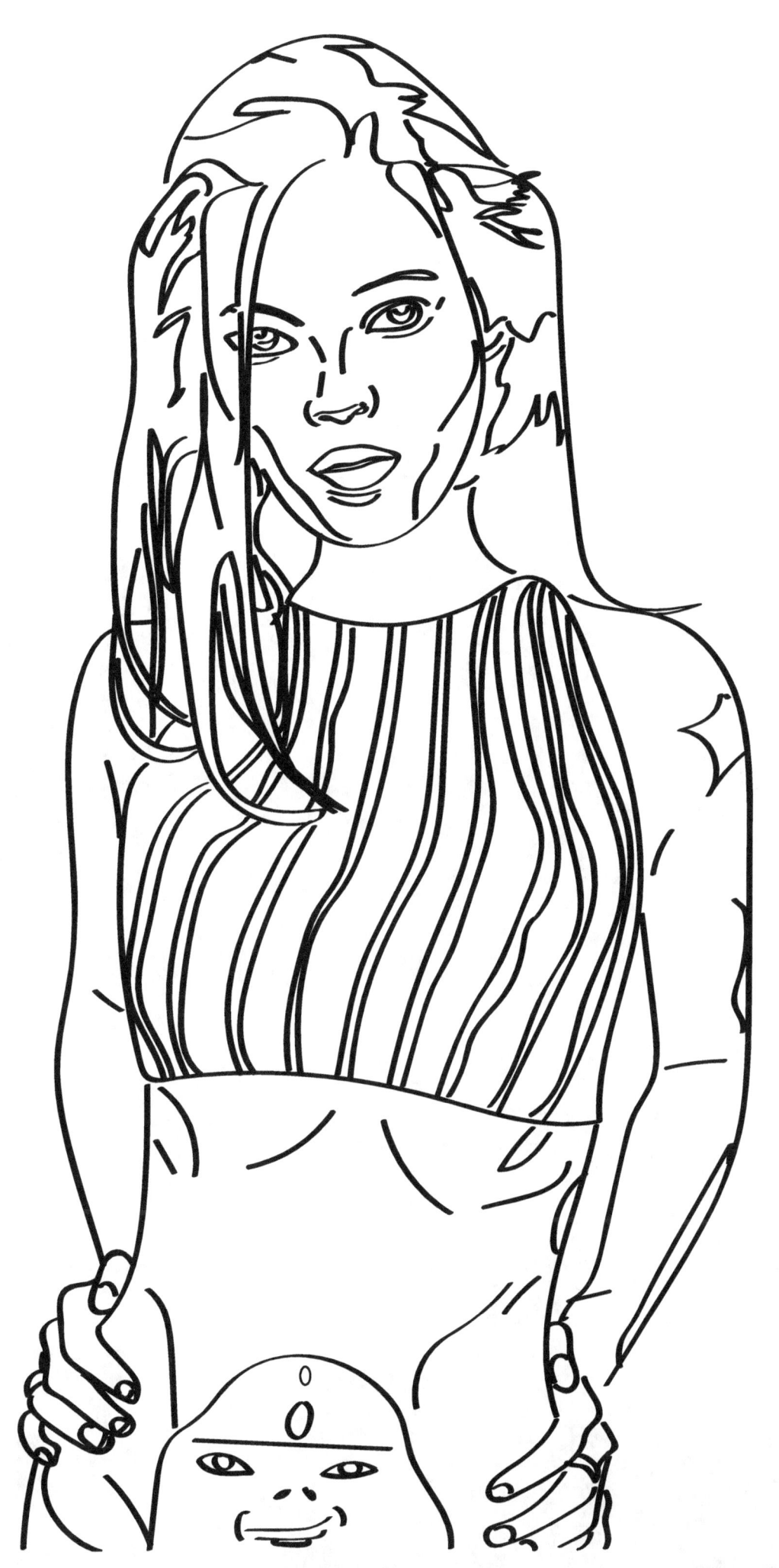

Dylan

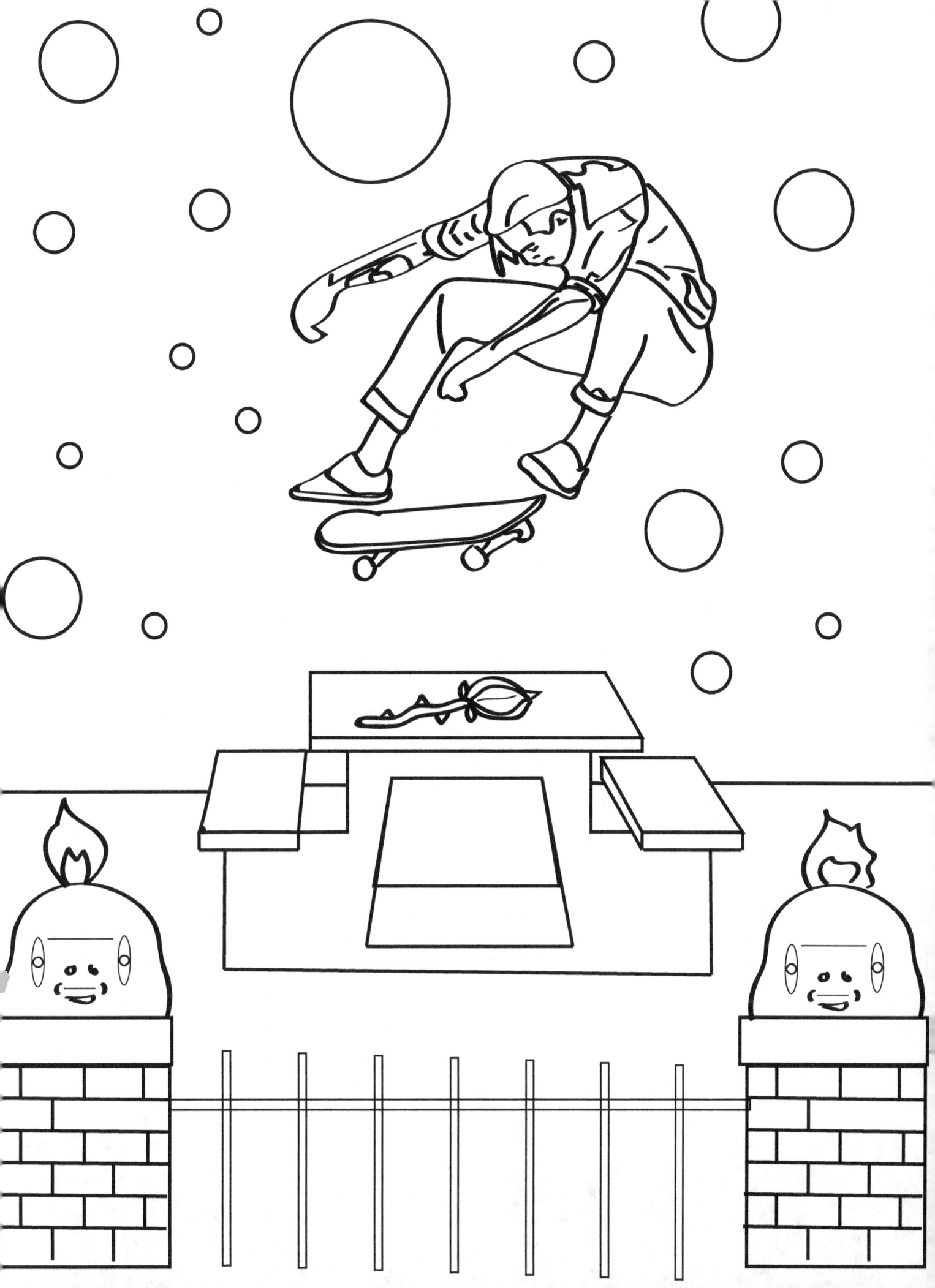

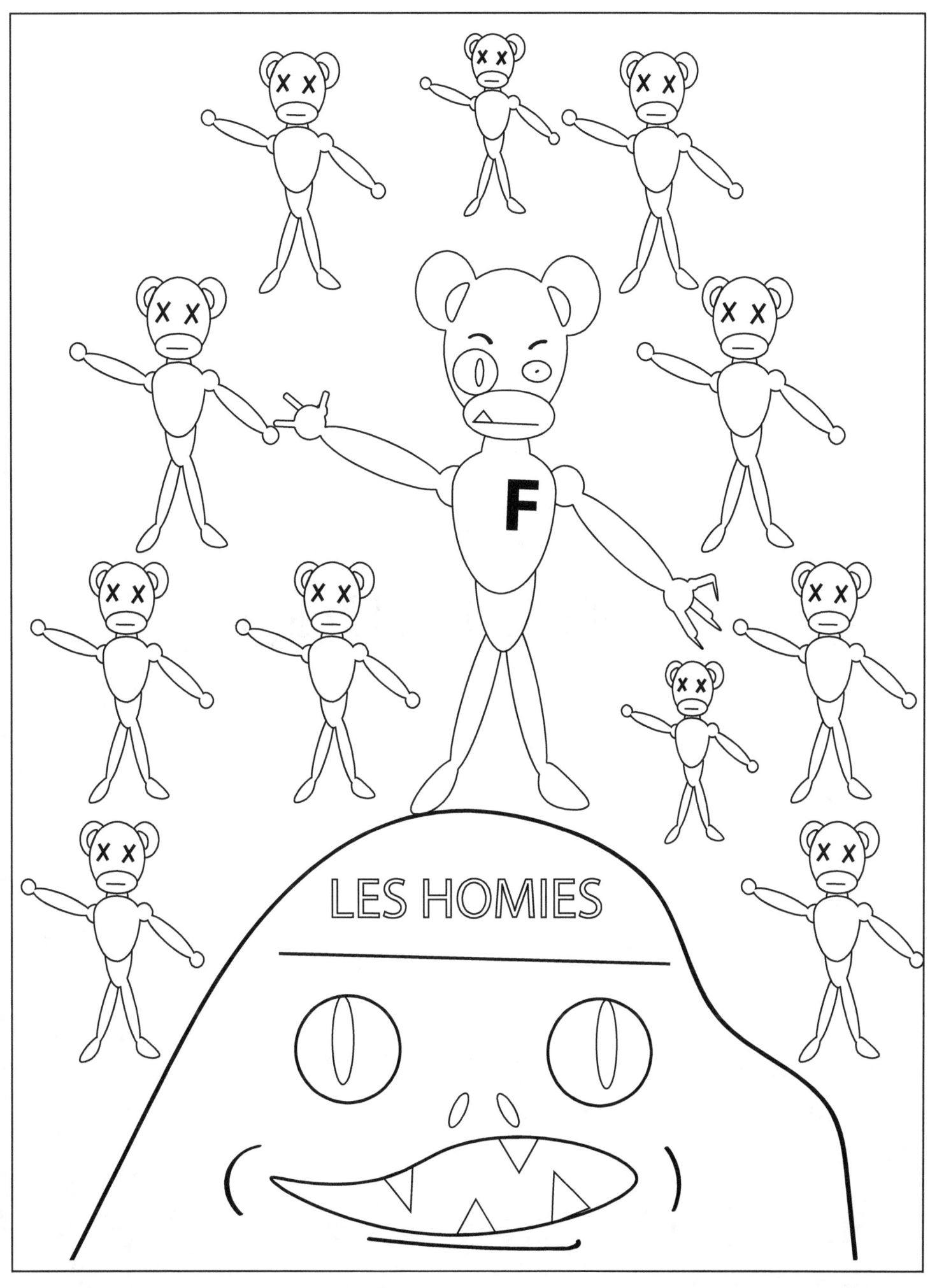

Walk The Dragon

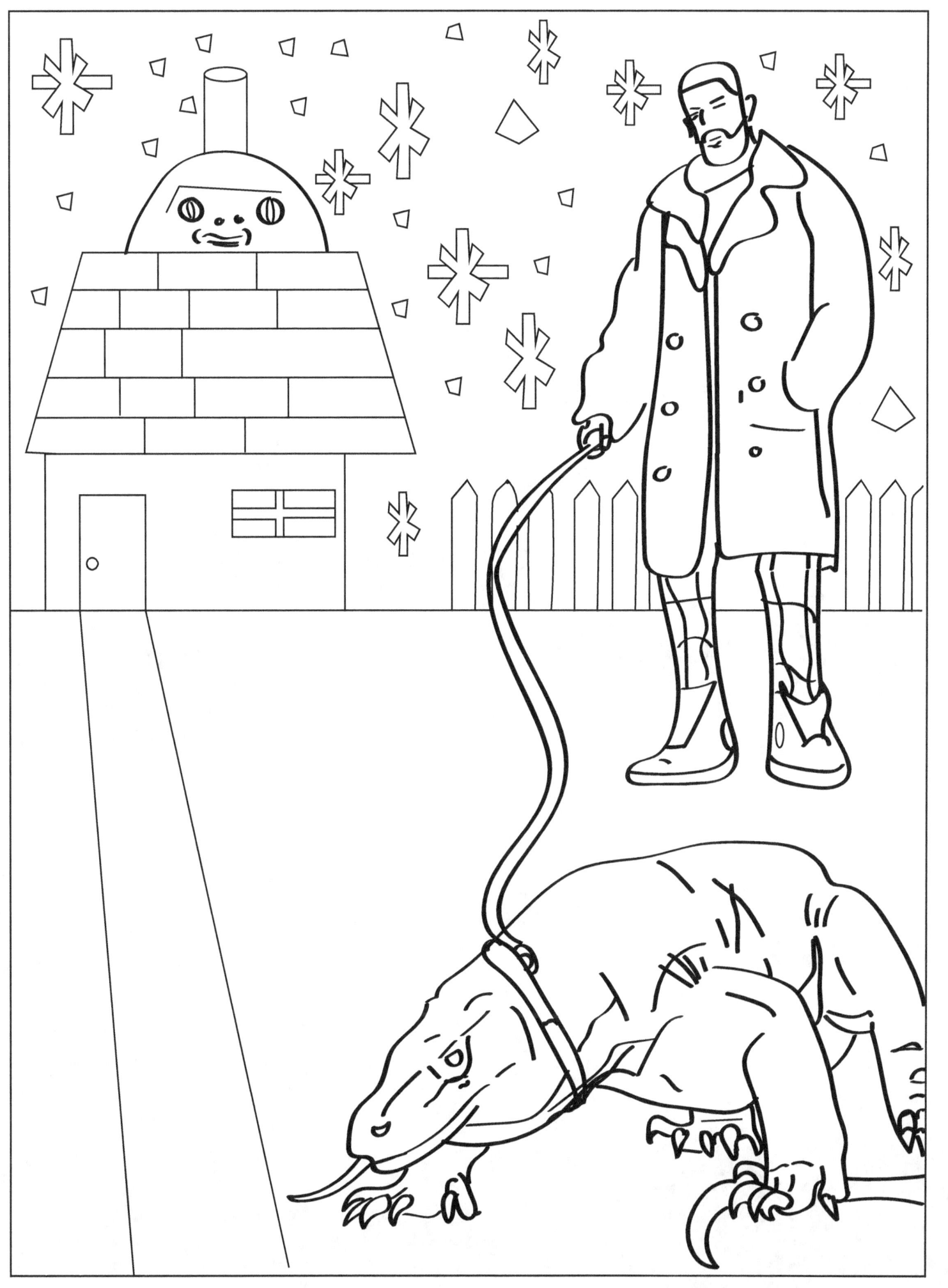

Bae by the Bay

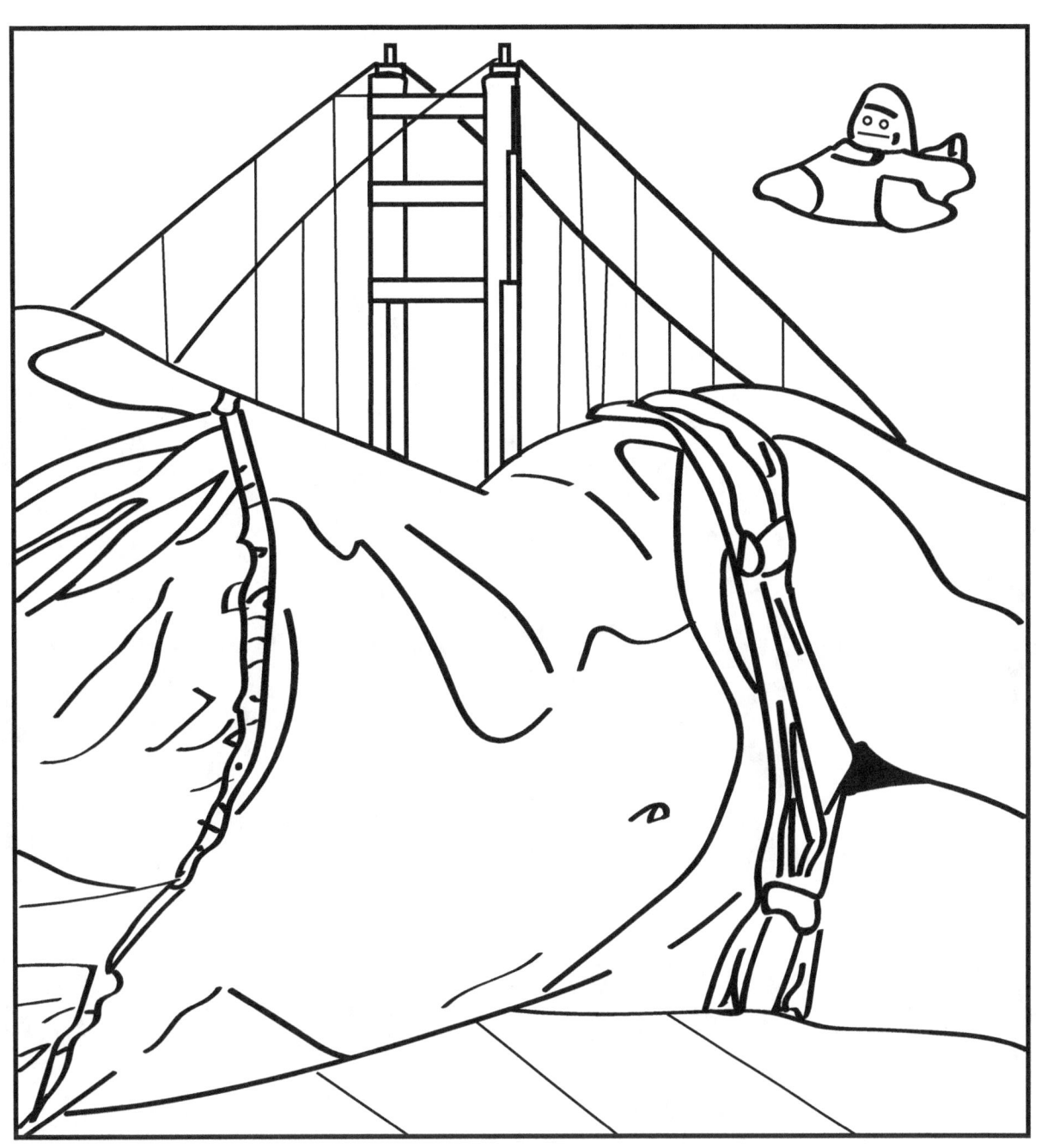

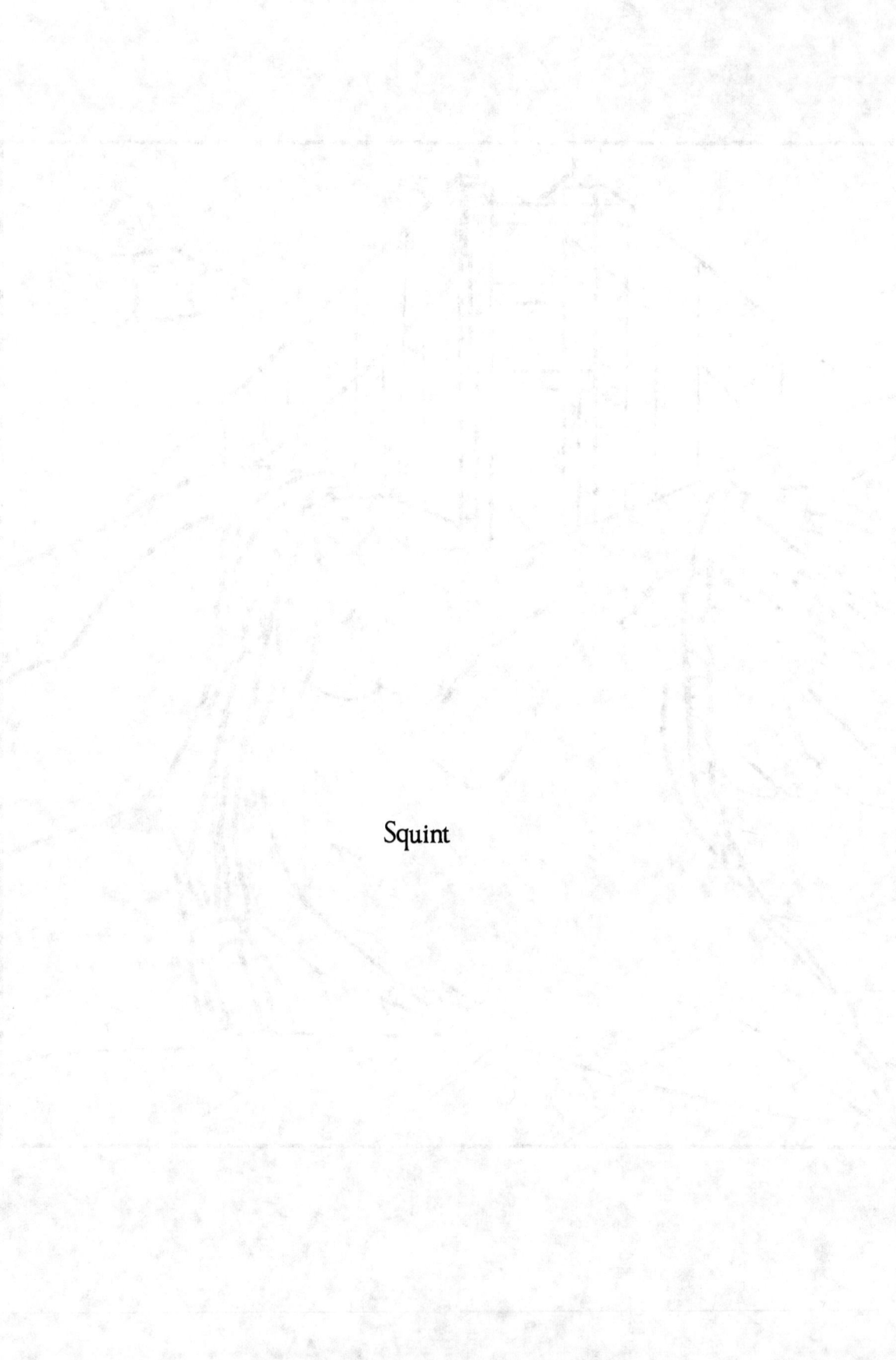

Squint

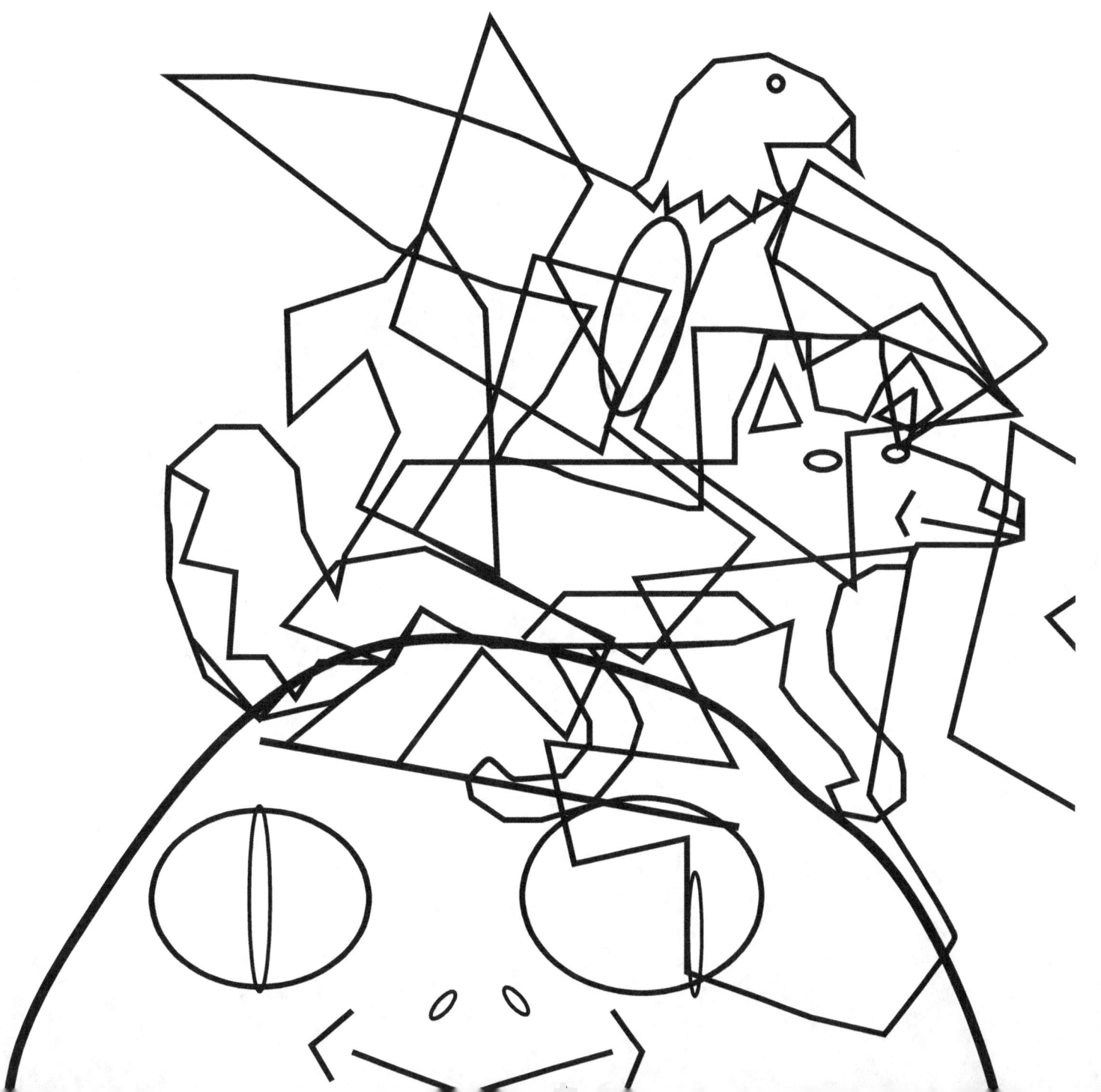

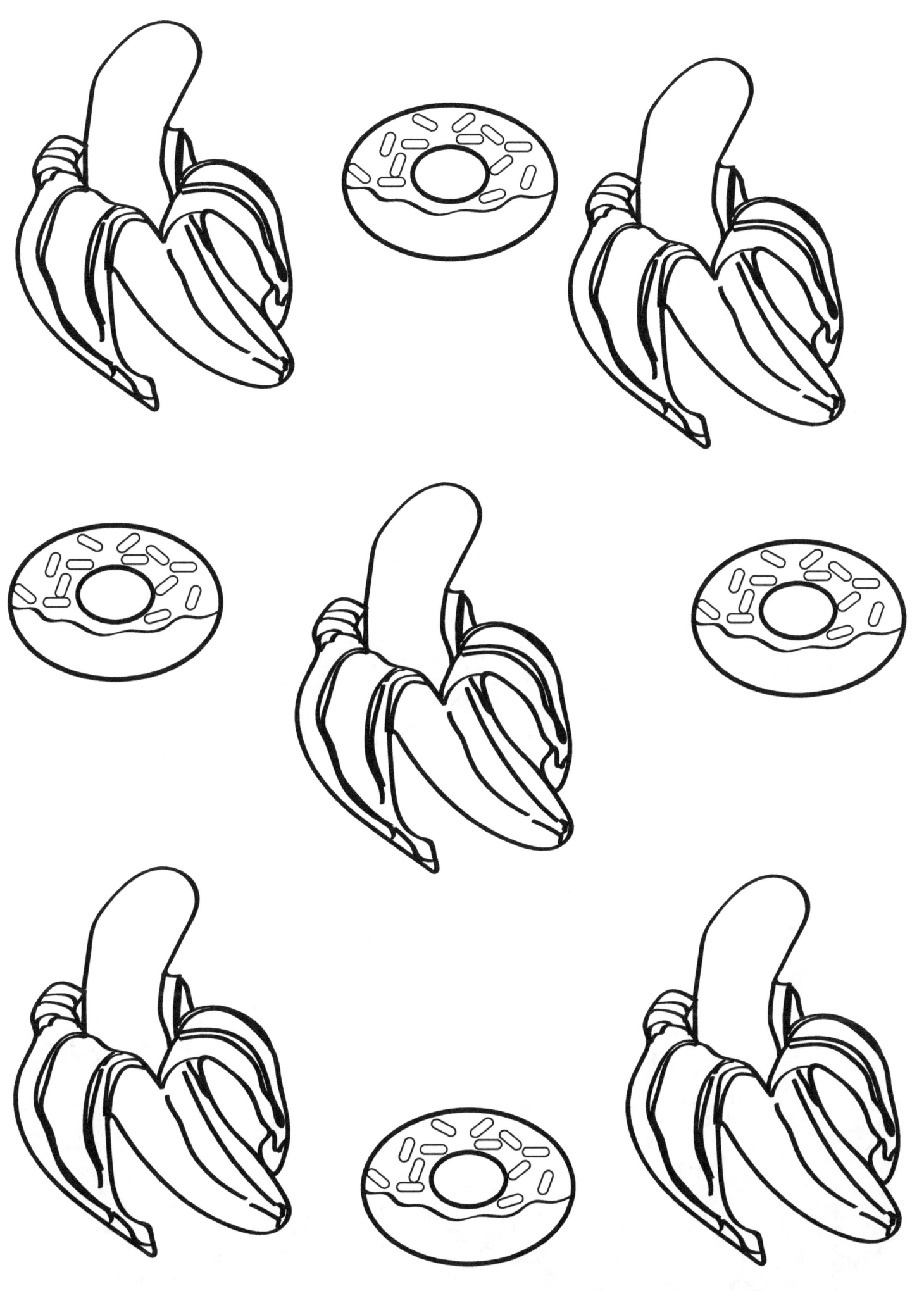

Sushi/Sushi/Flying/Sushi

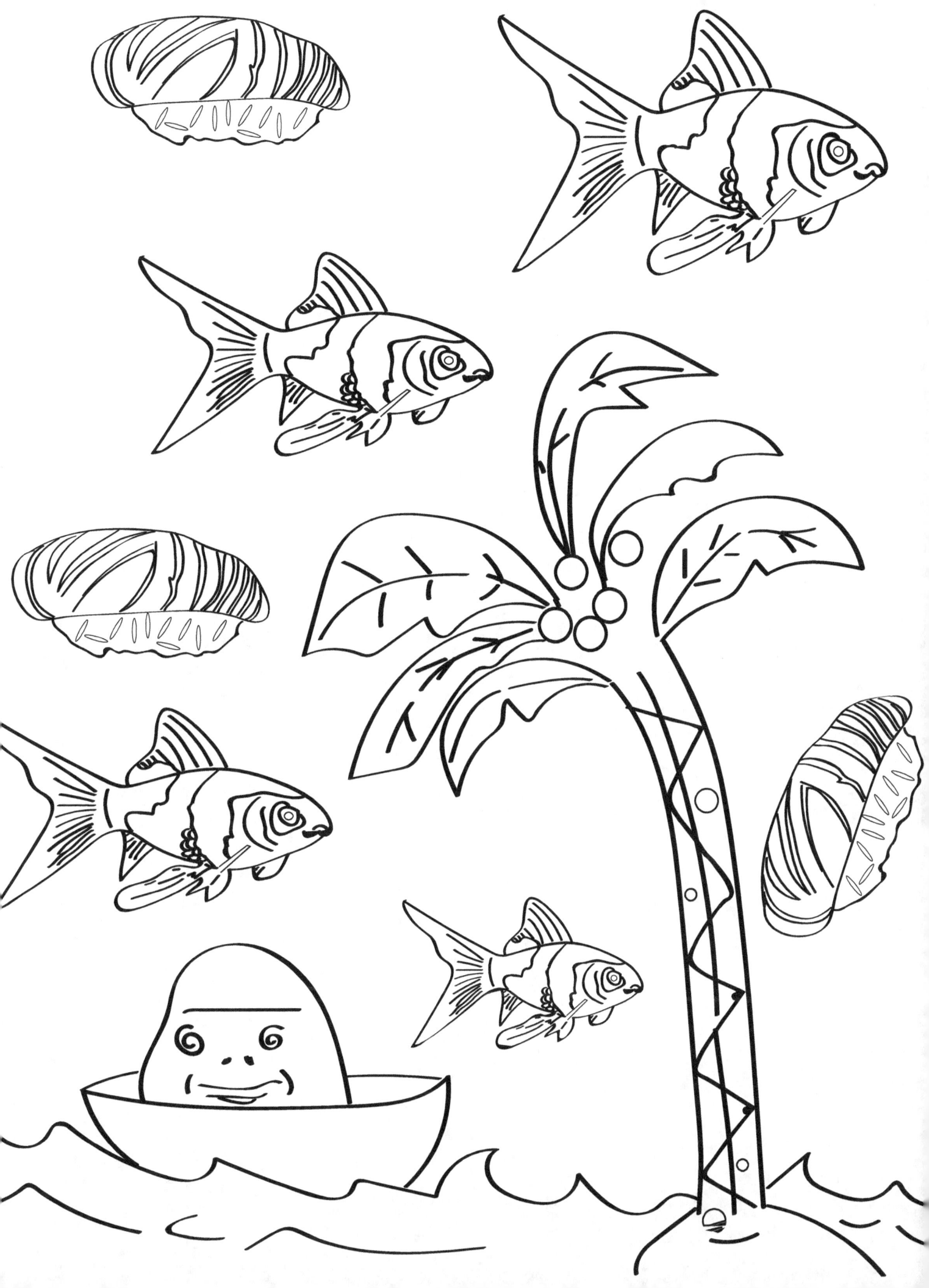

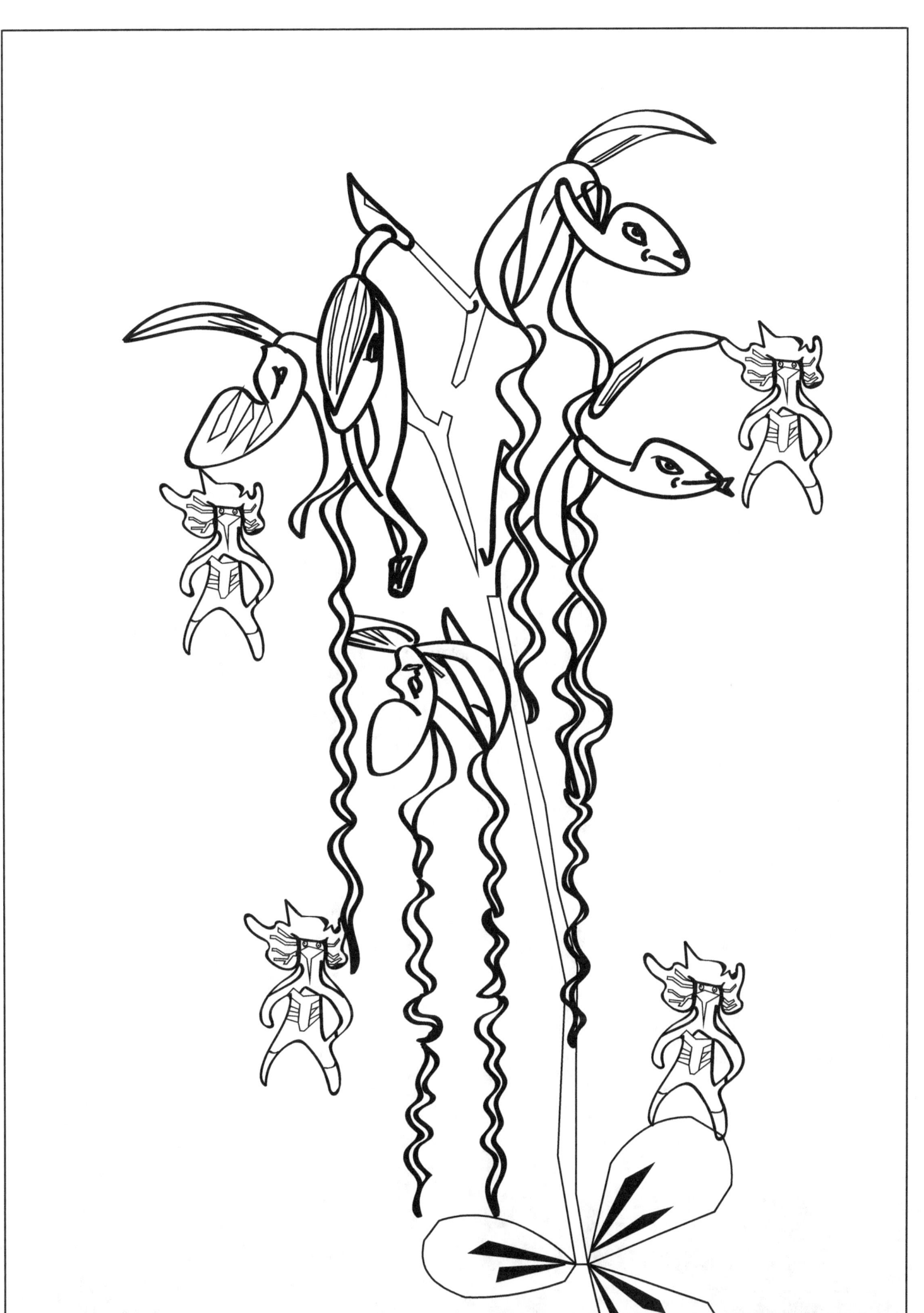

Champloo

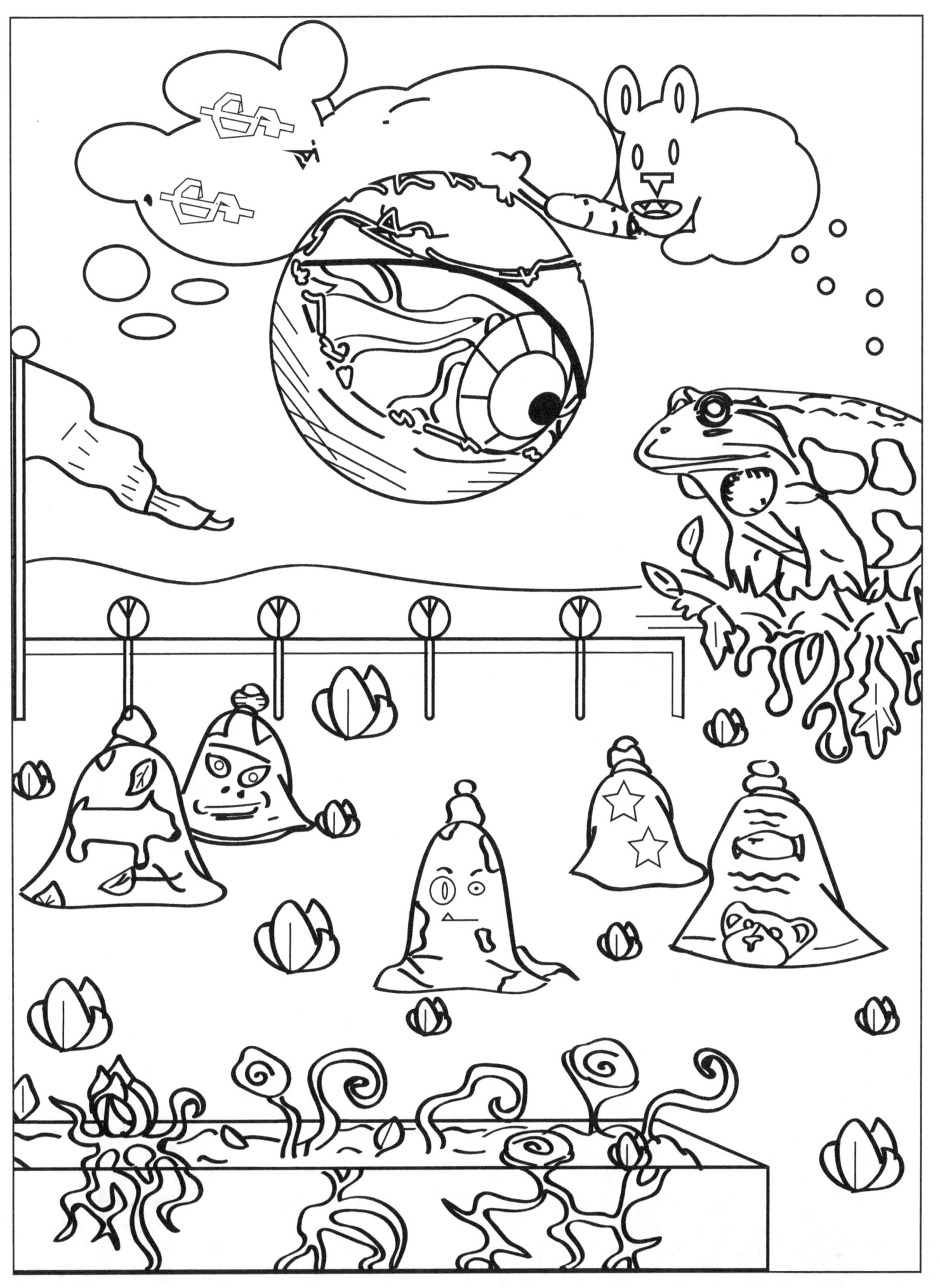

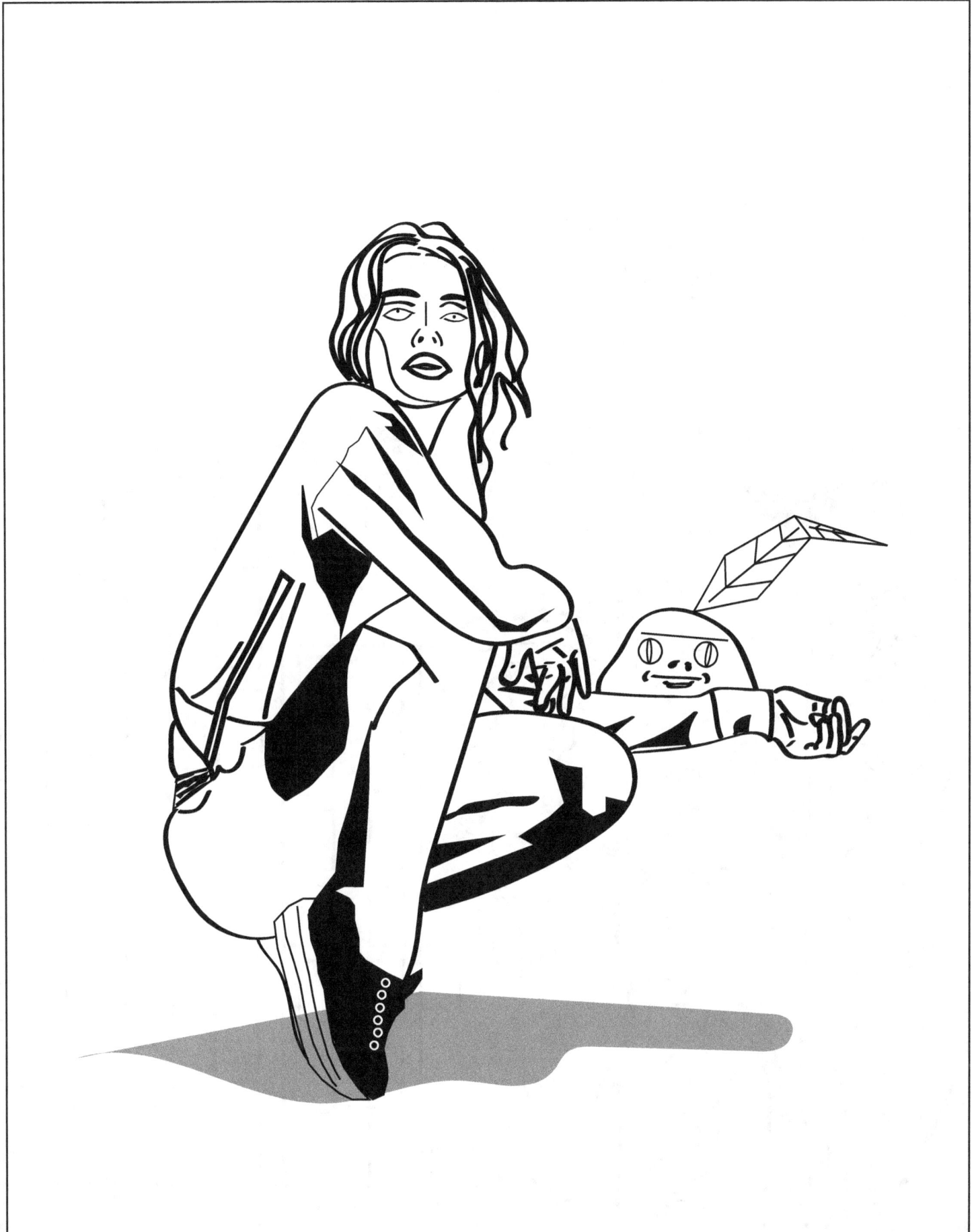

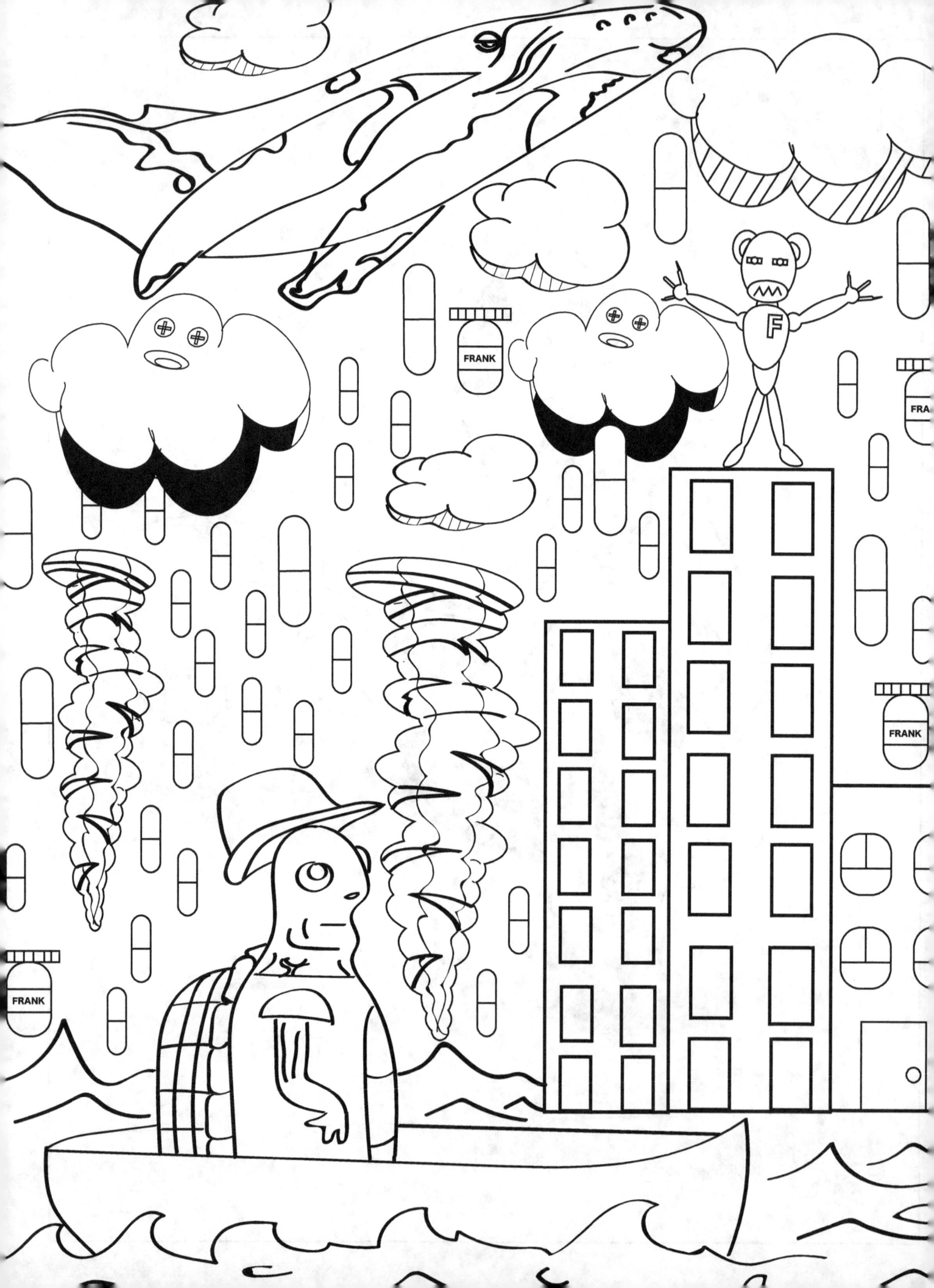

www.ingramcontent.com/pod-product-compliance
Lightning Source LLC
Chambersburg PA
CBHW081258180526
45170CB00007B/2474